The Scroll or the Sword?

The Sherman Lecture Series

The Sherman Lecture Series is an annual series supported by the Sherman Trust on behalf of the School of Oriental and African Studies, London, UK.

Edited by Dr Tudor Parfitt and Professor John Hinnels, School of Oriental and African Studies, London, UK.

The Scroll or the Sword? Dilemmas of Religion and Military Service in Israel

Stuart A. Cohen

Bar-Ilan University
Ramat Gan, Israel

Routledge
Taylor & Francis Group

LONDON AND NEW YORK

First published in 1997 by Harwood Academic Publishers.

This edition published 2013 by Routledge
2 Park Square, Milton Park, Abingdon, Oxfordshire OX14 4RN
711 Third Avenue, New York, NY 10017

First issued in paperback 2016

Routledge is an imprint of the Taylor & Francis Group, an informa business

---

British Library Cataloguing in Publication Data

Cohen, Stuart A.
 The scroll or the sword?: dilemmas of religion and military
 service in Israel. – (The Sherman Lecture series; v. 3)
 1. Draft – Israel – Religious aspects 2. Military art and science
 – Israel – Religious aspects
 I. Title
 355'.033'05694

 ISBN 90–5702–083–1

 Front Cover   Soldiers at prayer on the battlefield

ISBN 13: 978-1-138-98150-8 (pbk)
ISBN 13: 978-90-5702-083-4 (hbk)

For Tova and our children

Psalms 128:5–6

Contents

Acknowledgements   ix

Preface   xi

ONE   Decisions for War and Non-war:
        Classic and Contemporary Views   1

TWO   From Integration to Segregation:
        The Role of Religion in the IDF   37

THREE   The Religious Boundaries of
        Military Service in Israel   71

FOUR   Religious Military Units in the IDF:
        Sources of Pride and Subjects of Concern   105

Afterword   141

Index   145

Acknowledgements

Many people have helped me to write this book. First among them are Professor John Hinnels and my good friend Dr. Tudor Parfitt, both of the School of Oriental and African Studies at London University, whose invitation to deliver the 1996 Sherman Lectures originally prompted me to set down on paper the notes out of which the manuscript eventually emerged. Quite apart from extending warm hospitality, they also brought me into contact with an audience whose comments, and criticisms, provided the necessary stimulus for further research.

My other debts are of somewhat longer standing. For some years now I have been fortunate enough to conduct an annual post-graduate seminar on 'Israel and her Army' within the Department of Political Studies at Bar-Ilan University. It is a privilege to be able to express gratitude to all the participants, whose vigorous (sometimes heated) contributions have transformed a duty into a pleasure. Sincere thanks are likewise due to my colleagues at the BESA Center for Strategic Studies at Bar-Ilan, who provide so congenial an atmosphere for the study of Israeli security affairs in all their aspects. I am especially grateful to BESA's founder, Dr. Thomas Hecht, and Director, Professor Efraim Inbar, whose energetic leadership has propelled the institution to the very forefront of this particular field.

At a critical stage of research, funding was generously provided by the Ihel Foundation and Research Authority of Bar-Ilan University and by the Memorial Council for Jewish Culture in New York. Their support enabled me to benefit from the invaluable assistance of Ilan Suleiman and Kobie Green.

My greatest debt, and one impossible to specify, is to my wife Tova and our four sons. Always a source of encouragement, they have in this particular case also been a fount of knowledge and first-hand information. Flaws in the book are entirely my responsibility; whatever virtues it may possess are very much theirs.

Preface

The title of this book is derived from an ancient Jewish teaching, attributed to a certain Rabbi Eleazar of Modi'in, who lived in the land of Israel during the third century of the common era. As far as we know, Rabbi Eleazar was the first sage to take homiletic advantage of the alliteration of *safra* and *saifa*, Aramaic terms which literally translate (respectively) as 'a scroll' and 'a sword'. These two objects, he taught:

> "came down from heaven tied together. God said to Israel: 'If you observe the *Torah* [i.e. the Divine word of the Bible] which is written in the one, you will be saved from the other; if not, you will be smitten by it.'"[1]

A plain reading of this text leaves no doubt that its author intended to project a figurative contrast between two distinct spheres of human endeavour. Representing all canonical Jewish texts, the 'scroll' symbolizes the irenic pursuit of scholarship; by contrast, the 'sword' signifies martial action. The purpose of Rabbi Eleazar's aphorism, therefore, was to emphasize the need for the House of Israel to discriminate between these two very different paths to national and personal fulfillment.

Generations of traditional Jewish commentators have dutifully followed that prescriptive lead. Indeed, many extended the thrust of Rabbi Eleazar's teaching, transforming it into a proof text adduced in order to advocate the inherent superiority of a life dedicated to the devotional study of the entire rabbinic corpus. Typical, in this respect, is the interpretation provided by a Hebrew work entitled *Yefeh To'ar* ('Beautiful

---

[1] *Sifre: A Tannaitic Commentary on the Book of Deuteronomy* (trans. & ed. Reuven Hammer, New Haven: Yale University Press, 1986), parag. 40:7, p. 82. The passage also appears in: *The Midrash: Leviticus* (trans. J. Slotki, London: Soncino Press, 1939), parag. 35:6, p. 449; and *The Midrash: Deuteronomy* (trans. J. Rabbinowitz, London: Soncino Press, 1939), parag. 4:2, p. 90.

Countenance'), compiled in the 16th century by Rabbi Samuel Jaffe ben Isaac Ashkenazi of Constantinople, and which has since been printed as a marginal gloss on Rabbi Eleazar's adage in all standard editions of one of its principal sources. As portrayed by Rabbi Eleazar, writes Ashkenazi, the scroll and the sword do not simply depict the discretionary choices open to man. Properly understood, those two seemingly inanimate objects in effect convey value-laden concepts, and reverberate with connotations which are expressly Divine.[2] Because the *Torah* (Divine Law) is a 'tree of life' — indeed, is specifically referred to as such in Proverbs 3:18 — the 'scroll' denotes God's grace. On the other hand, the 'sword' signifies the Almighty's disfavour, a meaning evident ever since Adam and Eve were barred from re-entry into the garden of Eden by "a flaming sword which turned every way to preserve the way of the tree of life" (Genesis 3:24). It follows, therefore, that scholarly and military activities can never be reconciled. They are to be regarded as incompatible alternatives rather than equal imperatives.

Contemporary Israeli uses of Rabbi Eleazar's imagery tend to be entirely different. To an extent, that is hardly surprising. Modern political Zionism, the movement founded in the late 19th century with the express purpose of re-establishing "a Jewish homeland openly recognized, legally secured", constituted far more of a reaction to traditional Judaism than its extension. Motivated almost entirely by secular impulses, most early Zionists in fact self-consciously rebelled against the rabbinic precepts and practices which they diagnosed as being at least partially responsible for the depths of cultural stagnation and physical weakness into which their nation had sunk. This attitude of disdain towards so extensive a swathe of the Jewish historical

---

[2] *Yefeh To'ar* on *Leviticus Rabbah* ('The Midrash to Leviticus') 35:6. See also Samuel Eliezer Edels (1555–1631), *Hidushei Ha-Maharsha* ('Novellae') on *The Babylonian Talmud* (hereafter BT), tractate 'Avodah Zarah', folio 17b: s.v. 'Either the scroll or the sword'. Edels' commentary is appended to all standard Hebrew editions of the Talmud.

experience did not prevent Zionist spokesmen from invoking traditional Hebrew symbols, motifs and expressions when communicating with the audiences which they sought to galvanize into concerted political action. But it did result in a far-reaching exercise in displacement, now rendered 'countermemory'.[3] Far from simply adding new nuances to the cultural treasure-trove which they mined for polemic purposes, political Zionist pronouncements (even when articulated by observant Jews, as became the case once an expressly 'religious' wing of the movement was founded in 1902) tended to invest those sources with entirely new meanings, many of which blatantly contradicted their original sense and intention. So forceful was this process, and so conspicuous its success, that in several instances the traditional interpretations of passages of Jewish liturgy and homiletics have during the past century virtually disappeared from view. In colloquial discourse, certainly, they have been subsumed beneath a thick varnish of modern Zionist readings.

Such has been the fate of the aphorism attributed to Rabbi Eleazar of Modi'in, quoted above. Recent Zionist interpretations almost invariably turn that text inside out. Instead of being portrayed as contradictory entities, the scroll and the sword are projected as complements to each other. More explicitly, they are said to be intertwined rather than in conflict, and hence regarded as equally necessary for the survival of the modern Jewish state. In some cases, that effect is achieved by a sleight of the scribal hand. Only the first line of the teaching is cited; the codicil contained in the sentence commencing "God said to Israel..." is conveniently ignored.[4] In other instances, mat-

---

[3] Yael Zerubabel, *Recovered Roots: Collective Memory and the Making of the Israeli National Tradition* (Chicago: University of Chicago Press, 1995). See also: David N. Myers, *Re-Inventing the Pages of the Jewish Past: European Jewish Intellectuals and the Zionist Return to History* (New York: Oxford University Press, 1995).

[4] See the complaints to this effect expressed on the floor of the Kneset (Israel's parliament) in March 1983 by a representative of the ultra-Orthodox religious party, Agudat Yisrael, in *Kneset Protocol* (Hebrew), vol. 96 page 1826.

ters take an even more succinct and graphic form. Thus, the term '*safra* and *saifa*' (with each of those words inscribed on facing leaves of a bound book, and mounted by an army helmet) has been employed as a logo of the privately-funded Israel Institute of Military Studies, one of the country's most prestigious 'think-tanks' on security affairs. The same phrase, in this case accompanied by a sketch of two soldiers sword-fencing with pens in hand, also serves as the running title in the book review section of the Hebrew-language strategic studies journal *Ma'archot.* This has been issued since 1949 under the imprint of the Israeli Ministry of Defense, and is generally acknowledged to be by far the most authoritative of the Israel Defense Force's in-house publications.

Whichever the medium employed, the message is the same. Indeed, '*safra* and *saifa*' has become a slogan, used to communicate two separate meanings. Strictly speaking, one is instrumental: if they are to be successful, Israel's military operations must reflect the application of 'brain-power' as well as 'muscle-power' (a teaching also conveyed in the frequent citation of Proverbs 24:6: "Wisdom prevails over strength, knowledge over brute force; for wars are won by skilful strategy, and victory is the fruit of long planning"). The second meaning implied by the twinning of *safra* and *saifa* is still more extensive, and when contrasted with the traditional interpretation of Rabbi Eleazar's text, also far more revolutionary. In modern Israel, it implies, religious practice and military service are not anathemas. Rather, they make up two sides of the same coin and create a reciprocal dynamic. In this sense, the phrase encapsulates a particularly resonant vision of the dual nature of the new Jew's responsibilities. Duty-bound to serve his country as both a scholar and a soldier, he (and she) must endeavour to blend those charges and ensure that the possible tensions between them never preclude their joint fulfillment.

To what extent have the latter aspirations in fact been realized? Does the structure of Israel's armed forces indeed enable serving troops to harmonize their religious and their military obligations? Can their adherence to compulsory conscription be sustained at a time when increasing numbers of practicing orthodox young men are claiming exemption from the draft in order to pursue a scholarly vocation? Above all, to what extent is Israeli society equipped to face the challenge which might be presented to its stability by servicemen who could harness their martial expertise to ultra-nationalist religious zeal?

For many years, such questions — if ever posed — aroused only marginal public interest. Born into war in 1948, and thereafter subjected to persistent military threats to its survival, the new Jewish state wittingly (and in some accounts enthusiastically) adopted several of the characteristics conventionally associated with the notion of 'a nation in arms'.[5] The needs of national defence created a common patriotic denominator around which the religious and secular communities, and indeed all strata of society, could unite and rally. Hence, Israel's citizens determinedly closed ranks around their armed forces. Although otherwise resolutely committed to democratic norms and procedures, they also acquiesced in the liquefaction of many of the civil-military distinctions which are usually considered to be necessary hallmarks of western democracies.[6] At the apex of the Israeli social structure, for instance, the country's civilian and military elites forged a particularly intimate partnership, cemented by the ease with which senior officers often attained access to executive positions in either public service or the private sector on their retirement from active duty. Still more

---

[5] Uri Ben-Eliezer, "A Nation in Arms: State, Nation, and Militarism in Israel's First Years," *Comparative Studies in Society and History*, 37, (1995), pp. 264–285.

[6] Amongst the landmarks in the literature are: Amos Perlmutter, *Military and Politics in Israel. Nation-Building and Role Expansion* (London: Frank Cass, 1969); Dan Horowitz. The Israel Defense Forces: A civilianized military in a partially militarized society, in *Soldiers, Peasants and Bureaucrats* (eds., R. Kolkowicz and A. Korbonski; London: George Allen & Unwin, 1982), pp. 77–106; Yoram Peri, *Between Battles and Ballots: Israeli Military in Politics* (Cambridge: Cambridge University Press, 1982); and Rebecca L. Schiff, "Israel as an 'uncivil' state," *Security Studies*, 1, (1992), pp. 636–658.

extensively, a military ethos also pervaded Israel's wider social fabric. Military service in TZAHAL, the Hebrew acronym for the Israel Defense Force [IDF], became endowed with a ritualistic public status as the most meaningful of civic obligations, incumbent upon women as well as men and on middle-aged reservists as well as young conscripts. Moreover, in its corporate capacity as the guardian of national survival and as the custodian of national values, the Force constituted an essential ingredient of Israel's 'civil religion' and one of the principal vehicles for the dissemination of the new Jewish concept of 'statism'.[7] Largely as a result of all these circumstances, the dichotomies which traditional Jewish teachings had posited between religious practice and martial duty virtually disappeared from view. Instead, there prevailed a powerful aura of public consensus, which at times of military emergency became almost mystical. Embracing both religious and secular segments of Israeli society, that aura expressed the absolute priority of state security in the hierarchy of all interests, personal as well as national.

Those conditions no longer apply. As subsequent chapters in this book aim to demonstrate, they have in part been modified by ideological processes at work within the introspective world of religious Israeli Jewry. At this juncture, what needs to be noted is that they have also been undermined by a more widespread erosion in the status of many of the civic values and symbols, which were at one time considered axiomatic features of Israel's political culture.[8] Far from being immune

---

[7] Charles S. Liebman & Eliezer Don-Yehiya, *Civil Religion in Israel: Traditional Religion and Political Culture in the Jewish State* (Berkeley: University of California Press, 1983). On the evolution and implementation of 'statism': Mitchell Cohen, *Zion and State: Nation, Class and the Shaping of Modern Israel* (Oxford: Blackwell, 1987), esp. pp. 202–227.

[8] This is a central theme in: Dan Horowitz, & Moshe Lissak, *Trouble in Utopia: The Overburdened Polity of Israel* (Albany: SUNY Press, 1989); and *Israeli Democracy Under Stress* (eds. E. Sprinzak and L. Diamond; Boulder: Lynne Rienner, 1993), esp. pp. 255–359.

to that development, relationships between Israeli society and the IDF have been one of its most prominent victims. Whether those relationships might be re-formulated and, if so, how, now constitute major items of public concern, generating an uneasy debate which reverberates throughout the political framework. The ambience of uncertainty thus created warrants somewhat further elaboration, not least because it provides the context necessary for an understanding of the emergence (or, by the standards of traditional Judaism, the re-emergence) of tensions between the rival loyalties of religious precepts and military duties.

Although not an entirely linear development, the erosion of Israeli domestic confidence in the IDF has certainly been a cumulative and protracted process. In retrospect, its origins can probably be traced to the first days of the October 1973 'Yom Kippur' war, which erupted in circumstances which caused Israel's defence establishment to sway dangerously on the pedestal of infallibility that it had mounted so triumphantly during the Six Days' War of June 1967. The spectacular rescue of Jewish hostages at Entebbe in 1976, followed by the exemplary 'surgical' destruction of the Iraqi nuclear installation at Osiraq in 1981, did much to restore the IDF's own self-esteem, and certainly embellished its record of military accomplishment. Nevertheless, those successes exerted only a momentary braking effect on the depreciation in its public standing, which considerably accelerated thereafter. In part, this was due to the Lebanon War (1982–1985) and the *intifadah* (1987–1993) both of which proved to be embarrassingly protracted campaigns, each studded with evidence of operational deficiencies at all levels of command. Celebrating its fortieth birthday in 1988, the IDF discovered that its reputation had become severely tarnished.[9] Subsequently, the Force was further discredited by reports of sporadic training accidents, occasional abuses of human rights

---

[9] Avner Yaniv, *Politics and Strategy in Israel* (Hebrew; Tel-Aviv: Sifri'at Poalim, 1994), pp. 375–390.

in the occupied territories and financial corruption at some senior levels of military command.

As significant as the factual occurrence of such incidents is the degree to which they have been made public.[10] Throughout the first three decades of statehood, the Israeli media had followed a subservient policy of strict self-censorship with respect to all items of information falling within the broad compass of national security. Thereafter, however, it increasingly adopted a blatantly intrusive and censorious posture. So, too, did the courts and (in some respects more vociferously) parents and spouses of conscripts and reservists. Surveys of public opinion suggest that, notwithstanding such developments, the IDF still maintains its status as the most widely respected of all Israeli institutions.[11] Nevertheless, the emergence of a far less deferential attitude towards the Force remains one of the most conspicuous features of the nation's contemporary life. Informed observers, a category which encompasses senior military personnel as well as civilian academics, agree that the IDF has since the mid-1980s been progressively 'de-mythologized'. Men in uniform, once considered demi-gods, are now approached as mere mortals.

To this must be added the effect produced by the fundamental changes taking place in the country's overall security environment, especially now that Israel's peace treaty with Egypt (concluded in 1979) has been supplemented by a similar pact with Jordan (1994) and by a series of interim agreements with the PLO (1993–1995).[12] Open to various assessments, the quickened peace process has become a subject of acute domestic

---

[10] Gad Barzilai, *A Democracy in Wartime: Conflict and Consensus in Israel* (Hebrew; Tel-Aviv: Sifri'at Poalim, 1992).

[11] With the Supreme Court running a close second; see the 'indeces' periodically published by Efraim Yuchtman-Ya'ar and Yohanan Peres in *Israeli Democracy*, 1987–1991.

[12] For full references see the sources cited in: Stuart A. Cohen, "The Peace Process and its Impact on the Development of a 'Slimmer and Smarter' Israel Defense Force," *Israel Affairs*, 1/4, (1994), pp. 1–23.

dissensus, which on occasions takes violent forms. Welcomed as an opportunity to re-align national priorities by some, it is castigated as a slippery slope to ultimate catastrophe by others. The IDF has itself been drawn into the maelstrom of debate and can no longer sustain the image of a non-partisan institution entirely quarantined from conflicting political opinions. Instead, it has increasingly found itself forced to adopt a corporate stand on one side or the other of the public divide. Even strictly operational and organizational military concerns, once considered entirely beyond the pale of non-specialized scrutiny, now constitute battlegrounds of adversarial interpretations, many of which reflect blatantly ideological postulates.

This book seeks to explore the impact of that compound cluster of transformation on attitudes towards military service amongst various shades within the religious segment of Jewish Israeli society. More specifically, it aims to identify current areas of religious-military friction, principally by analyzing their sources and surveying their manifestations. To revert once again to the terms first employed by Rabbi Eleazar of Modi'in, attention will therefore be focussed on circumstances which are calling into question the continued viability of the accommodations originally intended to synthesize the scroll and the sword and ensure their co-existence.

As far as I am aware, no previous work has attempted that task. Several studies of contemporary Jewish society have investigated the ramifications of religious dissension in Israel from several angles and in considerable depth.[13] Yet, to the best of my knowledge, none have thus far extended the horizon of discussion to include a detailed study of relationships between Jewish religious communities and the IDF. That omission is

---

[13] Recent articles are collated in: "Israeli Judaism: The Sociology of Religion in Israel" (eds. S. Deshen, C. Liebman, M. Shaked), *Studies of Israeli Society*, vol. 7 (New Brunswick: Transaction Books, 1995), to which is appended a comprehensive bibliography.

regrettable. Quite apart from producing an incomplete picture, it also overlooks the most comprehensive of all Israeli national institutions, and certainly that which is most likely to be affected by a clash of conflicting emotions and ideals. The argument presented here adopts a different approach. The incremental intrusion of religiously-based tensions into the arena of military concerns, it suggests, cannot be relegated to the level of a marginal issue. Rather, that phenomenon warrants consideration as a particularly instructive barometer of the overall decline in the status of military duty as a rite of civic passage. It also reflects the appeal and variety of the new interpretations now being attached to the meaning of citizenship in a Jewish state. What those interpretations could involve in terms of commitment to military duty — and the extent to which military service might become contingent on the criterion of theological sanction — constitute some of the most fundamental of the many questions to which Israeli society is currently seeking a response.

Our own enquiry begins with an overview of the way in which contemporary religious discourse in Israel confronts the challenge of decisions to desist from war, placing that discussion within the context of traditional rabbinic enquiries into justifications for embarking on hostilities. Subsequently, attention moves to more specific sub-themes. Thus, chapter two examines the consensual role traditionally played by religion within the IDF, and thereafter identifies the strains to which that role is now being subjected. Chapter three analyses the differences in attitudes towards conscription evinced by the national-religious and traditional communities, and explores the theological justifications which each seeks to adduce. Finally, chapter four addresses the structure and possible behaviour of specifically religious units within the IDF, whose unique composition has given rise to suspicions that they might be particularly susceptible to military disaffection on ideological grounds.

ONE

Decisions for War and Non-war: Classic and Contemporary Views

Warfare played a crucial role in the formation of Jewry's national identity. Indeed, the earliest and most influential of Jewish traditions were formulated and transmitted against a background of almost incessant violence. As depicted in the Bible, the God of ancient Israel is, in addition to all else, the Lord of Hosts. Much of the scriptural record which begins with the book of Exodus and concludes with the last chapters of Chronicles concerns the campaigns waged in His name and fought by His chosen people. Many Psalms, similarly, are battle hymns and bear equal witness to the dominant role played by armed conflict in Hebrew society throughout the seven centuries spanning the Children of Israel's departure from Egypt and Judea's first experience of exile in Babylon.

The second Jewish commonwealth seems to have been likewise seeped in blood. Always surrounded by hostile enemies, the polity reconstituted by Ezra and Nehemiah around 500 bce had from the first to live by the sword. Moreover, it was for several generations ruled by the Hasmoneans, a dynasty which rose to power and sustained its sovereignty by the exercise of naked martial might. Not surprisingly, therefore, military values and associations colour the entire culture of the period. Their influence over contemporary apocalyptic thought was especially pronounced. The evidence to that effect long provided by the books of Maccabees, Jubilees and Judith has in our own century been corroborated by the discovery of the Qumran Scrolls, and in particular by that which bears the menacing title: "The War of the Sons of Light against the Sons of Darkness".[1] Consisting

---

[1] Edited by Yigael Yadin, and translated by B. & C. Rabin (Oxford: OUP, 1962).

1

of what amounts to a plan of campaign for the armies of the Messiah, the work graphically emphasizes the extent to which an aura of militarism had come to pervade Jewish religious perceptions, permeating even sectarians who inhabited the wastes bordering the Dead Sea.

I

And then, suddenly, the tenor of Jewish political behaviour and writings underwent a shift of seismic proportions. Pummelled into defeat by Rome in 70 ce, and even more savagely during and after the Bar Kokhba rebellion which broke out some six decades later, Jewry entered an extended period of what has recently been called "powerlessness".[2] The term, although requiring a hedge of numerous qualifications, nevertheless remains serviceable. Deprived any possibility of resorting to armed force, the attribute most commonly employed in order to audit national influence, Jews deliberately discarded their martial traditions. Instead, they drew inspiration from Zechariah 4:6: "Not by might nor by power but by My spirit, saith the Lord of hosts".[3] Their preferred response to persecution was flight and martyrdom, not resistance or revolt. Altogether, Israel became a non-combative people.

There were, admittedly, occasional deviations from that norm. Individual Jews are known to have fought under both the Cross and the Crescent in the great wars that raged between the Christians and Moors in medieval Spain. In later periods, some became adventurous soldiers of fortune, pursuing a profession of arms amongst such improbable company as the Spanish Conquist-

---

[2] David Biale, *Power and Powerlessness in Jewish History* (New York: Schocken, 1986), especially chapter 2: "The Political Theory of the Diaspora", pp. 34–57.

[3] For over two millennia, this verse has been incorporated in the scriptural readings for *Hanukkah*, the festival celebrating the victory of the Maccabees over their Seleucid foes in 135 bce. For a study of the recent use of that particular historical memory to re-create and disseminate an altogether more martial national myth, see: Eliezer Don-Yehiya, "Hanukkah and the Myth of the Maccabees in Zionist Ideology and in Israeli Society", *Jewish Journal of Sociology*, 34 (1992), pp. 5–24.

adors or Anglo-Indian troops of cavalry and infantry, and find-
ing fame at an exotic variety of unlikely locations, stretching
from the swamps of central America to the foothills of Afghani-
stan.[4] In the heartland of European Jewish settlement, others
(known to history as "cantonists") were in the second quarter
of the nineteenth century forcibly conscripted into the ranks
of the Imperial Russian army whilst still young children, and
thus condemned to perform military service on behalf of the
Tsar for periods which lasted for as long as 25 years. In yet
a fourth category, Jews eager to become fully accepted citizens
in their countries of residence voluntarily enlisted in the emerging
national armies of The Netherlands and the United States as
early as the late eighteenth century and, in ever-increasing
numbers, in those of France, Germany, Britain and Italy during
subsequent decades.[5] Nevertheless, all such instances were self-
evidently exceptional. Even when added together, the proportion
of Jews engaged in the profession of arms persistently lagged
behind that of the overall gentile average and never comprised
more than a fraction of the total Jewish population. More to
the point, not until the twentieth century does there exist any
reliable evidence that Jews — *qua* professing Jews and as a
collectivity — considered resorting to institutionalized violence
as a means of restoring their national independence or affirming their specifically religious identity.

Overwhelmingly, traditional Jewish thought underscored the
neglect of martial arts prevalent in traditional Jewish practice.

---

[4] For a blatantly polemical description of some of the most colourful characters see:
Fritz Heymann, *Der Chevalier von Geldern. Geschichten Juedischer Abenteuer*
(Koenigstein: Juedischer Verlag bei Atheneum, 1985 [reprint of the 1937 edition]).
Professor Dan Michman helpfully called this work to my attention.

[5] Salo W. Baron, "Review of History", in: *Violence and Defense in the Jewish Experience*
(eds. S. W. Baron and G. S. Wise; Philadelphia: The Jewish Publication Society of
America, 1977), pp. 3–14. The tangle of ritual and social difficulties thus generated
for the individuals and communities concerned can be glimpsed through the pages
of rabbinic correspondence. See: Yitzchak Ze'ev Kahana, *Studies in the Responsa
Literature* (Hebrew; Jerusalem: Mosad Harav Kook, 1973), pp. 163–194.

By the third century ce, at the latest, Jewish thinkers had begun to expunge virtually all memory of warfare from the national consciousness. Even the Bible, otherwise an inexhaustible well-spring of comfort and inspiration, was subjected to a process of re-interpretation, whereby tales of military valour and hero-ism were deliberately divested of their plain meanings. Thanks to the alchemy of early rabbinic exegesis, King David (for instance) was transformed from a warrior into a scholar; his band of champions underwent a similar metamorphosis from soldiers into students.[6] Yet more extensively, armed combat and its pursuit suffered what seems to have been deliberate scholarly neglect, even as topics of purely abstract or speculative analysis. Per-haps this was because the prospect that Jews might take up arms seemed so unrealistic; exile, after all, deprived them of an independent territorial base whose interests they might need to defend (or enhance) by a resort to organized force. Perhaps it was because political subjection in any case imposed its own stringent rule of discretionary silence. Such are the complex-ities of human motivation, that we can only speculate. But whichever the cause, the consequences remain the same. Military thought constitutes one of the very few spheres of intellectual enquiry to which neither Jews nor Judaism made any distinct-ive contribution of world-wide significance whatsoever for almost two millennia. Other civilizations can trace virtually unbroken chains of strategic traditions which stretch back to Sun Tsu, Kantichuya, Xenophon and Onasander, to Al-Tabari and Nasir-al-Din al Tusr or, at the very least, to Clausewitz, Jomini, Mahan or Liddel Hart. By comparison, Jewish culture since the early rabbinic era offers nothing but a lengthy void. Standard surveys of this particular sphere of human endeavour cite not one Jewish writer or source throughout the entire span which

---

[6] Stuart A. Cohen, "The Bible and Intra-Jewish Politics: Rabbinic Portraits of King David", *Jewish Political Studies Review*, 3 (1991), pp. 49–66.

stretches from Josephus, in the first century, until Bernard Brodie in the latter half of our own.[7]

Writing in the twelfth century, Judah Ha-Levi (circa 1075–1141), one of the greatest of all Hebrew poets and philosophers and a man decidedly imbued with proto-Zionist sentiments, openly bemoaned the decay of Jewry's martial ethos. Indeed, the argument that "if you [Jews] had the power you would slay" constitutes one of the only two debating points which Ha-Levi allows his spokesman for Judaism to concede to the "King of the Khazars" during the course of their imaginary theological dialogue.[8] No other exponent of mainstream Jewish religious belief, however, either anticipated or imitated that particular line of thought. On the contrary, all preferred to make a virtue out of necessity and to preach the religious efficacy of what the late Professor Yehoshafat Harkabi termed a policy of deliberate military inactivity and political passivity.[9]

One striking illustration of the degree to which that was so is provided by ancient and medieval rabbinic portraits of Bar Kokhba. The example is not chosen at random. Bar Kokhba, a figure reputed to have been endowed with extraordinary physical prowess and political charisma (his name translates as "son of a star"), lead the Jewish uprising against Roman rule in Palestine which erupted in 132 ce, just 60 years after the destruction of the second Temple. Although hard facts are difficult to disentangle from the soft tissue of fables, the basic history of his enterprise remains clear. Surviving sources (Gentile as

---

[7] E.g., Gerard Chaliand, *The Art of War in World History: From Antiquity to the Nuclear Age* (Berkeley: University of California Press, 1994).

[8] Judah Ha-Levi, *Book of Kuzari* (trans. H. Hirschfeld: New York: Pardes Publishing House, 1946), part 1, parags. 114–118. Significantly, the other point conceded by "the rabbi" is that Jews "fall short of their religious duty by not endeavouring to reach Zion" (part 2, parags. 23–24).

[9] Yehoshafat Harkabi, *Vision, No Fantasy. Realism in International Relations* (Hebrew: The Domino Press, 1982). The author, a one-time chief of IDF military intelligence and subsequently professor of international relations at the Hebrew University in Jerusalem, out-spokenly advocated an accommodation between Israel and the PLO as early as the late 1970s.

well as Jewish, numismatic as well as literary), confirm that Bar Kokhba's forces managed to re-capture Jerusalem and establish a revolutionary regime; Rabbi Akiva, the most illustrious religious teacher of the age, proclaimed him to be "King-Messiah". Thereafter, however, Bar Kokhba's fortunes collapsed. Within twelve months of the outbreak of the revolt, the Romans had ruthlessly counter-attacked and reoccupied most of the country. In the year 135 ce they overcame the last remaining stronghold of Jewish resistance. There followed an orgy of destruction. Over half a million Jews (including Bar Kokhba himself) were slaughtered; Jerusalem was utterly razed and vast portions of Judea deliberately turned into a wasteland.

Bar Kokhba has entered the contemporary Zionist pantheon as a symbol of heroic national resistance to foreign subjugation and as a role model of physical endeavour. His name was adopted by a Jewish athletic association founded in Berlin under Zionist auspices as early as 1900; Betar, the location of his last stand, became the designation of the youth movement founded by the Union of Zionist Revisionists in 1923. As Richard Marks has demonstrated, however, traditional Jewish interpretations had taken a far more ambivalent view of the entire episode with which Bar Kokhba is associated. Even those which acknowledged his virtues (and since he received the support of Rabbi Akiva, his virtues must surely have outweighed his vices), adamantly refused to identify him with the Messiah whose coming could alone could augur Deliverance. Instead, Bar Kokhba became:

"the prototypical false messiah and one of the great rebels of Jewish history.... The primary political lesson that premodern Jewish writers drew from the story was the lesson of political quietism. When most writers looked for the story's political meaning, they discovered a warning: it warned Jews not to seek national power by their own political, military efforts. Bar Kokhba usually stood as an example of forcing the end [i.e. of sinfully precipitate haste]."[10]

---

[10] Richard G. Marks, *The Image of Bar Kokhba in Traditional Jewish Literature: False Messiah and National Hero* (Pennsylvania: The Pennsylvania State University Press,

II

As early as the very first phase of their own enterprise, modern political Zionists became acutely sensitive to the handicaps inherent in the marginalization of warfare by Jewish political teachings. True, Theodore Herzl (1860–1904), who founded the World Zionist Organization in 1897, did not himself anticipate that his followers would have to reconquer their ancient homeland by force of arms. Hence, neither did he foresee any reason to nurture a martial ethos, required in order to ensure its defence. In fact, he blandly assumed that his proposed polity would require

"only a professional army, equipped, of course, with every requisite of modern warfare, to preserve order internally and externally." [11]

But Herzl's successors, especially once confronted with growing evidence of local Arab hostility to Jewish re-settlement, soon advocated the need for a far more radical approach. In this respect, as in so many others, the tone was set by the generation known to Zionist history as the "second *Aliyah*", the small but extraordinarily vibrant band of pioneers (most of whom emerged from a Russian revolutionary background), who arrived in Palestine between 1903 and 1914. Baldly summarized, their contribution to the transformation of Jewish political responses to the condition of chronic physical insecurity took two principal forms. One, necessarily the most basic, was the establishment of a network of embryonic self-defence organizations. A second, and in retrospect far more profound, was the adoption of a deliberately "activist" psychological and cultural profile. Rebelling against the posture of submissive

1994), p. 204. The rabbinic proof text for the admonition not to "force the end" is found in the BT, tractate *Ketubot*, folio 111a.

[11] Theodore Herzl, *The Jewish State* (originally published in London, 1895; reprinted by the Zionist Press, New York, 1946), p. 147.

"meekness" ingrained by centuries of exile, they sought to propagate an alternative ethos of organized militant struggle.

As Professor Anita Shapira has recently shown, when embarking on that course secular Zionists by and large invoked non-Jewish precedents. Although occasionally exploiting the warrior motifs and symbols of Israel's bellicose biblical past, most pre-State attempts to legitimize a national Jewish resort to force (whether in a "defensive" or "offensive" form) constituted adaptations of gentile terminology and models.[12] In their later versions, especially, they often simply echoed the slogans of secular, nationalist militarism which had become increasingly popular throughout continental Europe ever since the French revolution.[13] Religious Zionists, by contrast, faced a more difficult challenge. Compelled to defend Jewish militant activity in the terms dictated by the parameters of traditional Jewish discourse, they had to appeal more directly to indigenous canonical sources. To that end, even before the establishment of the state of Israel in 1948, they embarked on an atavistic intellectual quest, designed to rediscover — and, where necessary, to reconstruct — whatever the primary sources of Judaism might have had to say about warfare and its conduct. The purpose of the pages which follow is to follow the course of that particular intellectual exercise and to review the principal texts with which it has been concerned.

III

Following in the footsteps of all exponents of Jewish thought, Zionists and non-Zionists alike, we commence our enquiry with an analysis of the dicta transmitted by the towering medieval figure of Moses ben Maimon, better known in Jewish tradition as the RAMBAM and to the wider world of letters as Maimonides

---

[12] Anita Shapira, *Land and Power: The Zionist Resort to Force, 1881–1948* (New York: OUP, 1992).

[13] This argument has most explicitly been made in: Uri Ben-Eliezer, *through Gunsights: The Formation of Israeli Militarism, 1936–1956* (Hebrew: Tel-Aviv: Dvir 1995).

(1135–1204). The choice of that point of departure can easily be justified. Maimonides deserves to be regarded as the single most authoritative interpreter of traditional Jewish teachings on matters relevant to public as well as personal conduct; his code of Jewish law, the *Mishneh Torah* ("supplementary Torah", a title whose hubris looses nothing of its force from being taken from Deuteronomy 17:18), certainly constitutes the most comprehensive and systematic exposition of their content. Encompassing the entire corpus of instruction contained in the biblical, tannaitic, talmudic, and geonic literature, the *Mishneh Torah* welds into a single schematic whole, lucidly organized and fluently written, disparate and fragmented dicta otherwise widely scattered and obscurely buried in sources of varying accessibility. Although frequently disputed on individual matters of detail, and hence itself a base for great pyramids of commentaries and supra-commentaries, the Maimonidean code has entered the canon of Jewish literature as a benchmark. Its fourteen volumes, thematically sub-divided into 83 parts and 982 individual *halakhot* (literally "laws"), both summarize all previous Jewish teachings and provide a launching-pad for all subsequent elaborations.[14]

Maimonides' places his discussion of warfare in the very last volume of his code, which concerns the rights and duties of kings. This schema is itself instructive, underscoring the extent to which he regards the resort to organized violence as an essentially instrumental activity. Indeed, he goes as far as to state that:

"The prime reason for appointing a king was that he execute judgement and wage war, as it is written [I Sam. 8:20]: 'And that our king may judge us, and fight go out before us, and fight our battles'."[15]

---

[14] For a magisterial overview: Isadore Twersky, *Introduction to the Code of Maimonides (Mishneh Torah)* (New Haven: Yale University Press, 1980).

[15] *The Code of Maimonides*, Book XIV, "The Book of Judges", "Laws of Kings and Their Wars", 4:10 (trans. G. H. Hershman: New Haven: Yale University Press), p. 216.

By implication, therefore, warfare cannot be categorized as a sport, still less as a commendable way of life. Rather, and in the terms later made famous by Clausewitz, wars must serve defined political purposes. Furthermore, the shedding of blood can only be justified as an act of the last resort. Hence, basing himself on the authority provided by biblical injunctions and precedents, and on which early rabbinic teachings had already elaborated, Maimonides insists that acts of war be preceded by negotiation. Specifically:

"No war is declared against any nation before peace offers are made to it.... Once they make peace and take upon themselves the seven [Noachide] commandments, it is forbidden to deceive them and prove false to the covenant made with them." ("Laws of Kings and Their Wars", 6:1 and 3).

In the Christian political tradition, especially, the distinction between "just" and "unjust" wars generated lengthy and intricate discussions of what is known as the *jus in bello*. For the most part, their subject matter is the ethics of the behaviour of the combatants during the fighting and on the preservation — even during warfare — of a rigid differentiation between killing (which is legitimate) and murder (which is not).[16] Maimonides, and in his wake all mainstream Jewish texts, makes similar distinctions.[17] But that is not the sole issue of their concern. Significantly, Maimonides himself does not allude to such topics until he has conducted a detailed analysis of what legal parlance terms the *jus ad bellum*: the circumstances which sanction a resort to violence by authorized entities in the first place.

In the opening paragraph of the fifth chapter of his "Laws of Kings and their Wars", Maimonides distinguishes between two types of just war: one obligatory (in Hebrew: *milkhemet*

---

[16] In turn, these distinctions have led to an emphasis on noncombatant immunity and proportionality. See: Peter Ramsay, *The Just War* (New York: Charles Scribner's Sons, 1968) and Michael Walzer, *Just and Unjust Wars* (New York: Basic Books, 1977).

[17] Rav Shlomo Goren. "Combat Morality and the Halakhah", *Crossroads*, 1 (1987), pp. 211–232.

mitzvah; usually translated as a war fought for "a religious cause"); the other discretionary (*milkhemet reshut*, "an optional war"). This taxonomy is not a Maimonidean invention; its outlines can be discerned, albeit occasionally with variant terminology, in various portions of the talmudic corpus, which themselves draw on biblical citations.[18] Maimonides' contribution lay in the precision with which he refined the two categories and, in so doing, explored in systematic form their various nuances and implications. All subsequent rabbinic scholars, modern as well as medieval, follow his lead. As a result, the dichotomy between obligatory and discretionary wars has entered Jewish political discourse as a *topos*. Its purpose is to provide a gauge for measuring the religious validity of every branch of military activity with which all discussions of the *jus ad bellum* must necessarily be concerned.

IV

Several inferences might be derived from the distinction between wars which are obligatory (*mitzvah*) or discretionary (*reshut*). One is the extent to which each category obligates the mass of Jewish citizenry to participate in the fighting. Because this is so large a topic, and one which is particularly relevant to a review of tensions between religious precepts and military service in contemporary Israel, it will be analyzed in particular depth in chapter 3, below. More briefly, the remainder of the present chapter will focus on two other issues. First, the priority to be accorded to these categories of hostilities in strategic planning; secondly, the nature of the process by which, in either

---

[18] For details see: *The Talmudic Encyclopedia*, vol. 12, s.v. "Hovah" (Hebrew: ed. S. Y. Yevin: Jerusalem, 1967), pp. 464–7. The following discussion is also indebted to: J. David Bleich, "Preemptive War in Jewish Law", *Tradition*, 21 (Spring 1983), pp. 3–41; Efraim Inbar, "War in Jewish Tradition", *The Jerusalem Journal of International Relations*, 9 (1987), pp. 83–99; and Reuven Kimmelman, "The Laws of War and their Limitations" in: *The Sanctity of Life and Self-Sacrifice* (Hebrew; eds: Y. Gafni & A. Ravitzky; Jerusalem: The Zalman Shazar Center, 1992), pp. 233–254.

case, the decision to initiate combat must be preceded. Although often overlapping, these two latter topics nevertheless remain analytically distinct. Hence, they will here be reviewed sequentially.

(I) *Priorities in strategic planning*

Maimonides is explicit in ruling that strategic planning must accord priority to wars which fall under the obligatory classification. Thus:

> "The **primary** war which the king wages is war for religious causes.... **Thereafter**, he may engage in an optional war" (V:1).

This hierarchy flows almost inevitably from the illustrations which he provides for each of the two categories of hostilities. Optional wars, Maimonides writes, are those "fought against neighbouring nations to extend the borders of Israel and to enhance [the king's] greatness and prestige." In other words, they are campaigns of expansion, designed to serve the purposes of national or personal aggrandizement.[19] This facet of optional wars does not deprive them of all validity. Indeed, as later commentators were at pains to point out, demonstrations of military prowess constitute an essential component of statecraft. Thus, in his gloss on the *Mishneh Torah* (entitled *Lekhem Mishneh*), Abraham ben Moses Di Boton [1548–1588] explicitly argues that optional wars can be fought "in order that [the enemy] might fear him and not come against him". This is another way of saying that, as an instrument of foreign policy, even discretionary campaigns (provided they are successfully waged) can serve the essential purpose of both deterring putative aggressors and/or providing the polity with a "buffer zone" of territorial security. Presumably, other ration-

---

[19] The examples adduced by the Talmud are those conducted by the House of David in biblical times; see BT, tractate *Sotah*, folio 44b.

ales for optional wars can also be found.[20] Nevertheless, as justifications for the shedding of blood, all would be open to debate. For that reason, they are by the strict standards of the Maimonidean criteria, all considered subsidiary to the motives for which an obligatory war (*milkhemet mitzvah*) has to be fought.

In the opening to chapter five of his "Laws of Kings and their Wars", Maimonides provides three illustrations of the latter category of military campaigns:

"[i] The war against the seven nations [which inhabited Canaan prior to its conquest by Joshua]; [ii] that against Amalek [the tribe which, according to the biblical account, was the first to attack the Israelites after the exodus from Egypt; Exodus 17:8–13]; and [iii] a war to deliver Israel from the enemy attacking him."

He provides explicit biblical sources for only the first two of his examples (V:4 & V:5, respectively). The third ("to deliver Israel..." etc.) seems to be his own innovative appendage to the biblical code, ultimately justified by the generic prohibition against "standing aside while the blood of thy neighbour is being shed" (Leviticus 19:16) and the duty to ensure "that innocent blood be not shed in thy land" (Deuteronomy 19:10).[21]

It is tempting to regard "obligatory wars", as thus defined and illustrated, as a far broader category of military activity than that of "optional wars". After all, it could be argued, Maimonides' examples are just that: prototypes which serve to illustrate his typology. For instance, his reference to the "war against the seven nations" could be extended to any campaign

---

[20] As Inbar (op. cit., p. 86), points out, some of the traditional sources even adduce a domestic rationale. A telling passage in BT tractate *Sanhedrin* (folio 16a), for instance, relates that at least one of King David's campaigns was initiated in response to popular complaints of economic hardship. After considering — and rejecting — various remedies, David finally advised his people to "go and stretch forth your hands with a troop [of soldiers]". The implication is clear: the resort to force is a permissible means of relieving economic distress and thereby deflecting popular dissent.

[21] Rabbi Shlomo Goren, *Responding to War*, Vol. 1 (Hebrew; Jerusalem: Ha-Idra Rabbah, 1983), p. 36.

fought in order to attain (or restore) Jewish sovereignty over the Promised Land. Similarly, since "Amalek" has entered traditional Jewish demonology as a common personification of all evil, the commandment "to wage war against Amalek" could be extended to include any foe who might fit that depiction. In that interpretation, the illustration adduced by Maimonides might be projected as merely the opening round in an unending theological struggle between those who believe in Divine rule and those who do not.

In fact, traditional Jewish exegesis has in this respect been restrictive. Following Maimonides, the overwhelming consensus of rabbinic opinion is that both the war against the seven nations and that against Amalek are *sui generis*. Moreover, they were long ago consigned to a singularly suspended status. Neither now qualifies as an immediately relevant religious obligation. Rather, these two biblical commandments are depicted as frozen in time. Hence, whatever other sanction it may have, the reconquest of the Promised Land — in whole or in part — cannot be justified in terms of the instruction originally given to Joshua. Neither, similarly, can the commandment to wipe out Amalek vindicate a war of extermination against any other enemy. Maimonides does elsewhere comment that the king is commanded to "fight the battles of the Lord" (IV:10). But the very dissociation in his own code of this (deliberately ?) vague term from an Amalekite context is generally understood to underscore the degree to which the two are distinct. Some recent expositions which have suggested that the term "Amalek" might indeed be applied to present-day Israel's sworn enemies, and more specifically to her Arab neighbours, are as exceptional as they are notorious.[22] The overwhelming consensus of scholarly opinion argues that, there is very little indeed in Maimonides' writings, or those of any other mainstream rab-

---

[22] The most prominent instances are cited in Amnon Rubinstein, *The Zionist Dream Revisited: From Herzl to Gush Emunim and Back* (New York: Schocken Books, 1984), p. 112. Compare, however, the far more restrained view in Nachum Eliezer Rabinovitch,

binic commentator, which might legitimize a "Holy War" of conquest in response to a missionary impulse.[23]

Because it has thus refused to sanction an expansion of the circumstances to be included in the Maimonidean category of mandatory wars, modern Jewish jurisprudence has tended to impose strict limitations on the application of that term. In fact, the sole class of military activity to which the designation *"milkhemet mitzvah"* can now universally be assigned is what in current legal terminology would be termed a war of national self-defence. As much was recognized by some Israeli rabbinic authorities as early as 1948. Subjecting their few available sources to fresh forensic scrutiny, they were quick to point out the carefully circumscribed limitations prescribed by the Maimonidean *locus classicus.* Other than in the cases of Amalek and the seven nations, they noted, Maimonides endowed warfare with the status of a religious obligation only when fought "to deliver Israel from the enemy attacking him". This terminology necessarily excluded unprovoked offensive operations from the category of obligatory wars. It also implied that the enemy's action had to endanger an entire community. An attack on an individual Israelite would obviously necessitate a response (including, if possible, a violent response). But it could hardly be deemed sufficient cause to trigger a mandatory war, with all the responsibilities which that classification entails.[24]

As is apparent from even the most cursory of surveys, modern Israel's military practice has seldom conformed with the tidy

---

Melumdie Milkhamah: Responsa on Matters Concerning the Army and Security (Hebrew: Ma'aleh Adumim: Ma'alit, 1993), pp. 22–25.

[23] The contrast with Islamic tradition of a *jihad* is made explicit in Gerald Blidstein, *Political Concepts in Maimonidean Halakhah* (Hebrew; Ramat Gan: Bar-Ilan University Press, 1983), pp. 234–5. Compare: Abdulaziz A. Sachedina, "The Development of *Jihad* in Islamic Revelation and History", in: *Cross, Crescent and Sword: The Justification and Limitation of War in Western and Islamic Tradition* (eds. J. T. Turner and J. Kelsay; New York: Greenwood Press, 1990), pp. 3–50.

[24] Rabbi Isaac Herzog, *Chamber of Isaac* (Hebrew responsa; Jerusalem, 1972), part "Orah Hayyim", no. 39, pp. 96–99 (dated spring 1948).

categorizations of the rabbinic mind.[25] The principle of self-defence could most obviously (and justifiably) be applied during Israel's war of independence in 1948–9, when the infant state indeed seemed to be threatened with total destruction. By the same token, the term *milkhemet mitzvah* could similarly be deemed appropriate in October 1973, when the IDF was suddenly attacked in great force on both the Syrian and Egyptian fronts. Nevertheless, over the long haul, neither example deserves to be considered typical. For the most part, the situations compelling modern Israel to go to war have been less radical and hence, in legal terms, less clear-cut. Moreover, since the relevant circumstances have encompassed a wide range of military threats, each has necessitated an individual operational response. Although by no means invalidating the Maimonidean taxonomy, that development has necessitated a process of refinement, raising questions which can only be answered by the considerable exercise of interpretative manoeuvre.

Into which category of the Maimonidean formula are we to place, for instance, the *intifadah* (1987–1993), during which Palestinian insurgents deliberately resorted to what strategic jargon terms "low intensity warfare", restricting their attacks on IDF soldiers as well as Israeli civilians to barrages of stones and bricks thrown by groups of women and children? With what degree of force — if any — were Jewish troops then entitled to respond? The phrase "to deliver Israel from an enemy attacking him" is far too imprecise to supply an adequate answer to such queries, especially since the Hebrew term which Maimonides employs ("*ve-ezrat*") more precisely translates as "to assist" and can therefore denote a broad spectrum of force applications. Still less can the bland Maimonidean ruling serve as a clear guideline with respect to the timing of military action. Ostensibly, Maimonides seems to include within the category

---

[25] For a brief, but particularly sensitive, acknowledgement see: Rabbi Moses Feinstein, *Letters of Mosheh* (Hebrew responsa; New York, 1983), section "Hoshen Mishpat", no. 78, p. 149 (dated autumn 1979).

of an obligatory war only a "reactive-defensive" campaign, launched once the enemy attack has commenced. But is that the sole contingency to which the rubric of mandatory hostilities might apply? Where would he place a "pre-emptive" war, undertaken in anticipation of threatened enemy aggression, such as was launched by the IDF against Egypt in both the "Sinai campaign" of October 1956 and the Six Days' War of June 1967, or against the PLO in the Lebanon in both "Operation Litani" (March 1978) and "Operation Peace for the Galilee" (June 1982)? [26] And what would his ruling be in the case of a "preventive strike", such as the Israeli air bombardment of Iraq's nuclear installation in 1981, launched in order to destroy a putative enemy's war-making potential some time before the threat actually materializes?

There is no doubt that Jewish law provides a general sanction for military action in each of these cases. Nevertheless, beneath the exterior of that apparent *carte blanche* lurk the sort of imponderables over which Talmudists have always loved to fuss. Some concern the nitty-gritty of religious practice: How much latitude do troops engaged, for instance, in a pre-emptive strike enjoy with respect to violations of the Sabbath? Others, however, involve issues which are far more fundamental. Do "pre-emptive strikes" or even "pre-emptive wars" qualify as obligatory (*mitzvah*) actions? Or are they merely discretionary (*reshut*)?

(II) *The Decision-Making Process*

Supposedly hard-nosed strategists of the modern "realist" school tend to scoff at the relevance of such questions. Altogether, they argue, the juridical dimensions of war taxonomies must be subordinated to the ultimate authority of national interest and to the horribly quantifiable calculus of mass destruction.

---

[26] Bleich, "Preemptive War in Jewish Law", esp. pp. 9–12.

Moral philosophers and legal experts can merely provide *ex post facto* justifications for whatever courses of action the state chooses to pursue. That is not a position available to a system of thought which approaches military matters (as all others) from a perspective based on religious foundations, and for which *a priori* distinctions between different categories of hostilities therefore constitute a vital test of their validity. Jewish teachings are particularly stringent in this regard. Far from relegating differences between obligatory and discretionary wars to the realm of mere academic speculation or legal quibble, Jewish traditions transmute that distinction into a litmus test of executive prerogatives. On this point, Maimonides is, again, absolutely clear:

"For a *milkhemet mitzvah*", he writes, "the king need not obtain the sanction of the court. He may at any time go forth of his own accord and compel the people to go with him.

But in the case of a *milkhemet reshut*, he may not lead forth the people save by a decision of the court of 71". ("Laws of Kings and their Wars", V:2).

To put matters another way: only in cases of obligatory campaigns do rulers possess the prerogative to reach unilateral decisions with regard to mobilization and the initiation of hostilities. Discretionary wars require a far more elaborate and decentralized process.

One possible explanation for that distinction is operational. An obligatory war, especially if occasioned by a direct enemy attack, is likely to require immediate military action. Needing to make urgent decisions on the spur of the moment, the ruler simply might not possess the time to go through all the time-consuming motions of constitutional consultation. But no such extenuating circumstances will apply to discretionary wars, fought "to extend the borders of Israel and to enhance [the king's] greatness and prestige", when considerably more leisure will presumably be available. In such cases, the formalities can be respected without in any way jeopardizing state security. If anything, it is precisely the health of the body politic which mandates that they be most scrupulously observed. The biblical books of Kings provide abundant evidence of the destructive havoc which can easily result from over-hasty decisions to go to war. Hence, any process which might delay the process and permit time for reflection possesses an intrinsic value which is as much political as humanitarian. Don Isaac Abrabanel (1437–1508), a renaissance figure who was deeply involved in the politics of decision-making in Spanish, Portuguese and Italian city courts and who also found the time to compile an elaborate commentary on the Bible, made this point with exquisite ingenuity. In his exegesis of Deuteronomy 20:3, which admonishes Israelites not to "tremble" before war, Abrabanel noted that the Hebrew term there employed, "hafez", can also mean "hasten". This *double entendre*, he suggests, is deliberate, and constitutes a warning of the possible penalties of reckless dispatch in such matters.[27]

To this must be added, secondly, a broader constitutional consideration. Maimonides, it will be recalled, identifies the body which the ruler has to consult before embarking on a discretionary war as "the court of 71." He refers, without doubt, to the agency which Josephus, the New Testament and various Talmudic texts all term "the Great Sanhedrin". For over a century now, modern scholarship has struggled to synthesize these various sources and thereby reconstruct the precise composition and powers of that body. Did it function as a royal council? Was it a priestly court? Or did it serve as a legal chamber in which Pharisaic scribes sharpened their debating skills?[28] None of these doubts troubled Maimonides at all. Adhering solely to the traditions preserved in the talmudic sources at his disposal, he depicts the Great Sanhedrin as a political-cum-religious agency, composed of seventy one sages, each an acknowledged expert in the Divine law of whose elucidation they were all masters.

---

[27] Inbar, "War in the Jewish Tradition", p. 96.
[28] See, e.g., Elias Rivkin, "Beth Din, Boule, Sanhedrin: A Tragedy of Errors", *Hebrew Union College Annual*, 46 (1975), pp. 181–199.

Although thus composed of essentially spiritual authorities, the Maimonidean "court of 71" constitutes much more than a clerical assembly. Its sphere of jurisdiction, while certainly encompassing religious ritual, is not limited solely to that domain. Hence, it does not fit the image of a representative of "Church" interests, which are distinct from those of "State". Rather, as depicted by Maimonides, the court of 71 is the engine of all Jewish government, embodying the means whereby civic as well as spiritual relationships might be structured and regulated in accordance with God's original teachings to Israel. Its functions, moreover, are just as wide as its mandate. Besides constituting the polity's supreme judiciary and legislature, members of the court of 71 also enact two other governmental roles. First, together with kings and priests, they form an integral part of the executive branch.[29] Second, they also possess a representative capacity, which derives from their character as the embodiment and enunciators of a broad national will.[30]

The latter two capacities of the court of 71, participant in the executive process and spokesman for national opinion, explain the different roles which it plays in the decision-making process prior to declarations of war. By definition, an obligatory campaign requires no authorization from this body, or any other. The fact that wars thus categorized as *mitzvah* enact explicit Divine commands constitutes the only possible mandate which could possibly be required. By contrast, a *milkhemet reshut*, precisely because of its religious discretionary character, does demand specific license.[31] Troops cannot be ordered to sacrifice their lives simply in order to satisfy the arbitrary will of kings; neither can they be commanded to shed the blood of

---

[29] No administrative action is constitutional unless kings, priests and prophets participate jointly in the decision-making process. See Stuart A. Cohen, *The Three Crowns: Structures of Communal Politics in Early Rabbinic Jewry* (Cambridge: CUP, 1991), esp. pp. 18–20.

[30] Blidstein, *Political Concepts*, pp. 58–61; and Bleich, "Preventive War", pp. 23–25.

[31] Hence, the suggestion that *milkhemet reshut* might best be rendered a "licensed" or "sanctioned" war. Bleich, "Preventive War", p. 35 fn. 7.

other human beings without a prior process of consultation which canvasses the opinions of non-monarchical elites. Not until the twentieth century did strategic thought in the west fully appreciate the extent to which victory in battle might hinge on consensus, both within society at large and at the apex of government.[32] The role allotted to the court of 71 in the countdown to a discretionary war suggests that, in this respect, ancient Jewish traditions were more prescient. Indeed, a direct line can be traced between the teachings which they contain and the weight attached in contemporary analyses to the importance of public support as a component in modern Israeli strategic doctrine.[33]

(III) *The Changing Agenda*

By the late 1980s, committed religious Zionists could be excused for assuming that, as far as the decision-making process required for war initiation was concerned, contemporary rabbinic thought had largely succeeded in making up for lost time. Although several particulars still needed to be clarified, most of the foundations for an adaptation of the classic rulings on warfare to the conditions of modern statehood were by then firmly in place. In minute (and sometimes obsessive) detail, the technicalities had been worked out by the time-honoured and laborious rabbinic process of exegetical analysis and textual review.

Much of this labour had been conducted in semi-privacy, and through the traditional medium of written "responsa" (in Hebrew: *teshuvot*) which halakhic authorities addressed to individual questioners in reply to their precise enquiries. How-

---

[32] Michael Howard "The Forgotten Dimensions of Strategy", *Foreign Affairs*, 57 (Summer 1979), pp. 975–86.

[33] Moshe Lissak, "Civilian Components in the National Security Doctrine", in: *National Security and Democracy in Israel* (ed. A. Yaniv; Boulder: Lynne Rienner, 1993), pp. 55–80.

ever, since a large proportion of such texts were subsequently published, they have now entered the public domain. Easily accessible (not least by virtue of the fact that many have been transferred to CD-Roms[34]), the responsa materials constitute an invaluable epistolary storehouse, providing a comprehensive a survey of the sort of religious queries which the novel condition of modern Israeli warfare was thought to pose. Do all IDF operations come under the category of obligatory wars? If so, to what extent might conventional Sabbath regulations be rescinded by serving soldiers and by non-combatants? Which portions of the daily prayers does a soldier have to repeat should he discover that he has inadvertently fallen asleep during the public service? How might religious troops fulfil the commandment to reside in a temporary booth during the festival of Tabernacles? Are they permitted to camouflage the white ritual fringes attached to their shirts? Most painful of all, what is the marital status of wives whose husbands are reported missing in action?

To the historian, the heterogeneity of questioners is just as informative as is the range of their questions. The line of greetings which, by convention, precedes each individual responsum reveals that many constitute replies to rabbis, who have sought advice from their scholastic peers and superiors. In several instances, however, the enquiries emanate from younger soldiers, and even groups of prospective conscripts, who possess no particular academic credentials. For that very reason, the tone of the reply tends to be more specifically pitched. Typical of this *genre*, and selected here because of both its style and its early date, is a responsum which Rabbi Isaac Herzog (1888–1959;

---

[34] See the index to the *Global Jewish Data Base*, published by Bar-Ilan University, (Israel, 1995). Most of the responsa relevant to military matters is buried in the body of those texts, which for the most part are concerned with the more conventional fare of rabbinic discourse. Only very recently have compilations of responsa been expressly devoted to the subject to hand. For an example see: Nachum E. Rabinovitch, *Responsa on Matters Concerning the Army and Security* (above n. 22).

Israel's [Ashkenazi] Chief Rabbi) addressed to some members of the religious youth movement *Ezra* in the spring of 1948. The correspondents were evidently eager to volunteer for service in defence of the soon-to-be-established state. But before doing so they asked for clarification on six specific items of sabbath observance. In reply, they did not merely receive dry legal guidance. They were also provided with a particularly stiff dose of aggressive spiritual encouragement.

"And once a person has entered into combat he must place his faith in Israel's fount and saviour in times of trouble. He should know that it is on behalf of the Divine Name that he is making war and endangering his life. Hence, he must neither fear nor be afraid nor think of his family... but concentrate entirely on war.... Moreover, the blood of all Israel hangs around his neck, and if he does not fight with his entire heart and soul it is as though he shed everyone else's blood.... But one who fights with full heart and fearlessly, and solely with the purpose of sanctifying the Divine Name, is assured that he will suffer no harm. He will build a true house in Israel ... and merit the life of the world to come."[35]

In parallel, another interesting development occurred. Rather than waiting to be asked to give religious rulings on matters of military concern, several Israeli rabbis took the initiative and compiled innovative compendia of their own. Clearly intended for a much wider audience than the readers of responsa literature, such works generally adopt a thematic approach and seek to encompass the entire gamut of religious dilemmas which military service might pose, moral and ritual alike. The trend was set as early as 1941, when Rabbi Abraham Yeshayahu Karelitz (1878–1953; the "Hazon Ish", see below p. 89), a scholar renowned throughout the orthodox Jewish world for his piety and learning, issued *Sefer Mahaneh Yisrael* ("The Book of the Camp of Israel"), a small tract containing spiritual guidance for Palestinian Jewish soldiers fighting in the British army during World War II. But since 1967, especially, that pioneering effort has been succeeded by an ever-increasing stream of more detailed

---

[35] Isaac Herzog, *Chamber of Isaac*, no. 37. Herzog attributes these words to his predecessor in office Chief Rabbi Abraham Isaac Kook.

compilations, many written by rabbis themselves in possession of military experience at first-hand. The sheer volume makes this corpus almost as impossible to digest as it would be to overlook. As one's eye roves along the relevant shelves in the library, the most prominent titles in what has now become an extended chain of authoritative exposition immediately command attention: *Mishpat Ha-Milkhamah* ("The Law of Warfare", 1971) by Shemaryahu Arieli; *Ha-Hayil ve-ha-Hosen* ("Soldiering and Immunity", 1989) by Joshua Hagar-Lau; *Pe'ilut Mivtza'it Be-Tzahal Al Pi ha-Halakhah* ("Operational Activities in the IDF According to the Halakhah", 1991) by Isaac Jakobovitz; *Ha-Tzavah Be-Halakhah* ("The Army in the Halakhah", 1992) by Isaac Kaufman; *Darkei Milkhamah* ("The Ways of War", 1996), by Mordechai Frumer; and, most impressive of all, Shlomo Goren's *Meishiv Milkhamah* ("Responding to War", 1983) — three fat volumes of instruction and polemic by the IDF's first Chief Rabbi.

Such has been the expansion and somewhat hectic tempo of modern Israel's military experience, that all such works have soon outlived their shelf-life and therefore periodically required up-dating. That process has itself generated a further stratum of literary commentaries. These have most commonly appeared in the pages of learned journals which explicitly chronicle intra-rabbinical efforts to come to terms with modern Jewish statehood. Particularly informative, and especially influential, have been three such publications: *Ha-Torah ve-Ha-Medinah* ("The Torah and the State"), thirteen issues of which appeared between 1949 and 1962; *Barkai* (six issues since 1983); and *Tehumin*, which has appeared annually since 1980.[36] Packed with intricately argued articles of resounding erudition, each volume in these series has created an additional link in an extensive com-

---

[36] Some of the articles in *Tehumin* have been translated into English, and appear in an annual entitled *Crossroads: Halacha and the Modern World*, published since 1987 by the Zomet Institute in Gush Etzion. Where available, I refer in the notes to the translations.

munications network, building up a body of religious law and instruction in areas which had lain uncharted for centuries.

Considering the paucity of recent precedents for the autonomous exercise of Jewish power, especially in the sphere of military conduct, the achievement was considerable. Understandably, and justifiably, it generated an ambience of self-congratulation. In its reconstructed form, the framework of halakhic rulings concerning warfare (generically known as *dinei milkhamah*) seemed by and large to satisfy the traditional scholastic criteria of both coherence and comprehension. Thanks to the exercise of considerable cerebral agility, even the cast of characters required for a decision to embark on hostilities had been appropriately re-named. Prior to the foundation of the State, Herzog's predecessor as Ashkenazi Chief Rabbi, Rabbi Abraham Isaac Kook (1865–1935), had reasoned that the existence of the public authority which Maimonides had invested in "the king" was not dependent on the physical presence of a personage bearing that rank. Properly understood, he argued (on the basis of an admittedly obscure item of medieval rabbinic commentary), monarchy embodied national sovereignty and emanated from the people. Hence:

"When there is no king... the prerogatives of the laws [associated with kingship] revert back to the people in its entirety. It seems, furthermore, that the authority of kingship is assumed by any leader who represents the nation and administers its affairs for the common good."[37]

Within less than four decades of independence, and after already experiencing several large-scale military campaigns, a constellation of rabbinic worthies within the national religious community were prepared to be still more specific. Modern Israel's democratically elected government, they argued, had self-evidently inherited the war-making powers which Maim-

---

[37] Abraham Isaac Kook, *Mishpat Kohen* (Hebrew; responsa relating to the Land of Israel; Jerusalem: Mosad Harav Kook, 1966), no 144. Originally dated 1916, this responsum was first published in 1937. On Kook's influence, see below pp. 79–80.

onides ascribes to Hebrew monarchs. As the embodiment of a national consensus, the *kneset* [parliament] likewise possesses at least a portion of the authority which the Maimonidean code had invested in the "court of 71".[38]

V

As religious Zionism approaches the sixth decade of national independence, this mood of self-assurance and inner certainty is steadily being undermined. Amongst the several reasons, probably the most salient, and undoubtedly the most ironic, is the accelerated pace of the current peace process between Israel and the Palestinians. The train of events initiated by the conclusion of the first Oslo accords in September 1993 not only altered the trajectory of the country's military and diplomatic history. More specifically, it also shifted the entire ground of halakhic discourse. Instead of being required simply to refine their reconstruction of the traditional code on war initiation, rabbinic experts and spiritual guides were now called upon to address the other side of the coin. Under what circumstances might an independent Jewish government be empowered to *desist* from going to war and, in an effort to conclude peace, even relinquish sovereignty over territories thereto under its control — including portions of the Land of Israel itself?

On a purely theoretical level, such questions were raised almost as soon as the Six Days' War of June 1967 was over.[39] But the need to grapple with them as concrete issues arose when the time came to implement the 1979 peace treaty between

---

[38] Rabbi Shaul Israeli, "The Contemporary Jurisdiction of the Laws of Kingship" (Hebrew), *Ha-Torah ve-ha-Medinah*, 2 (1950), pp. 76–88 and Rabbi Shlomo Goren, *The Torah of the Sabbath and Festivals* (Hebrew; Jerusalem: The World Zionist Organization, 1982), p. 451.

[39] For examples of early enquiries, and responses, see Yehudah Shaviv (ed.), *Land of Inheritance* (Hebrew; Jerusalem: The Mizrachi Organization, 1977), pp. 119–120 and 130.

Israel and Egypt. In accordance with the terms of that document, Prime Minister Menachem Begin's government (of which representatives of the National-Religious Party [the MAFDAL] formed an essential component) in 1982 ordered the dismantlement of the Jewish settlement of Yamit on the fringes of the Sinai desert. In response, the settlers and their supporters, the vast majority of whom identified with the tenets of religious Zionism, formed a "Movement to Stop the Withdrawal", compelling the government to order the IDF to resort to physical force.[40] At stake, as one observer subsequently noted, was far more than a question of diplomacy or even of security. The clashes which ensued encapsulated a conflict:

"between the idea of an essentially secular state, one based on the rule of law and endowed with a 'legal-rational' legitimation by its citizens, and the idea of a Jewish religious state, based on 'traditional' legitimation, derived ultimately from God."[41]

The theological and political passions aroused by the evacuation of Yamit did not evaporate with the conclusion of that particular episode. If anything, subsequent developments generated even greater heat, which in turn lead to increasingly insistent calls for rabbinic guidance. One significant phase in that process occurred during the *intifadah*, when — so Israeli settler communities in Judea and Samaria charged — the government deliberately curtailed the IDF's freedom of military response to local Palestinian attacks on Jewish lives and property. A second wave of such calls was generated during the protracted negotiations between Israel and the PLO, which resulted in a series of interim agreements between 1993 and

---

[40] For a virtually blow-by-blow account, see: Yaacov Bar-Siman Tov, *Israel and the Peace Process, 1977–1982: In Search of Legitimacy for Peace* (Albany: SUNY Press, 1994), esp. pp. 155–242. For a personal account of the feelings aroused amongst the settlers, see: Aliza Weisman, *The Withdrawal* (Hebrew: Bet El; Sifri'at Bet El, 1990).

[41] Erik Cohen, "The Removal of the Israeli Settlements in Sinai: An Ambiguous Resolution to an Existential Conflict", *Journal of Applied Behavioral Science*, 23 (1987), pp. 140–141.

1995, and which are scheduled to reach a "final settlement" by 1999.

From the perspective of both previous Zionist practice and traditional Jewish teachings, the importance of the situation created by the transformation of Israel's security posture lies as much in its novelty as in its substance. Therein, too, lies a key to the dilemma which it poses for exponents of orthodox national-religious thought. True, contemporary religious Zionists can look back to a fairly lengthy history of political accommodation and even of military moderation. In 1900, for instance, their intellectual forbears had been ready to accept "Uganda" as a possible alternative to a Jewish homeland in Palestine, arguing that the immediacy of the physical need for a territorial refuge, whatever its location, had to take precedence over their sentimental attachment to the Holy Land. Largely on the same grounds (albeit much more grudgingly) religious Zionist leaders had in 1937 been prepared to accept the Palestine partition proposal then momentarily submitted, and soon withdrawn, by the British government. Most strikingly of all, between 1936 and 1939, the overwhelming majority had also acquiesced in the policy of "restraint" (*havlagah*) advocated, and adopted, in the face of persistent Arab terror by the majority of the Zionist *Yishuv*.[42] But none of these precedents can easily be applied to the present situation. It was one thing to have justified political compromise and/or military self-denial at a time when Jewish control over Palestine was still partial, tenuous and subordinate. Simply to re-cycle the same arguments now that there exists a powerful and independent state, equipped with an army which wields military dominion over the entire Holy Land, is an entirely different matter.

---

[42] Itamar Wahrhaftig, "The Position of the Rabbis in the Controversy over Partition (1939)" (Hebrew), *Tehumin*, 9 (1988), pp. 269–301; and Eliezer Don-Yehiya, "Religion and Political Terrorism: Orthodox Jews and Retaliation during the 1936–1939 'Arab Revolt'" (Hebrew), *Ha-Tzionut*, 17 (1993), pp. 155–190.

The need for a re-assessment is further compounded by the absence of any clear policy guidelines in the canonical texts to which religious Jews almost instinctively turn when faced with novel situations. If anything, the announcement that the Rabin government had decided to reduce the IDF's presence in "the territories", some of which it agreed to transfer to the control of the Palestinian Authority, exposed an embarrassing lacuna in the existing halakhic code. To the extent that the classic formulators of Jewish law devoted any attention at all to matters of military strategy, they had done so on the understanding that the only issues requiring attention concerned the initiation of hostilities and their conduct. By contrast, deliberate self-restraint from an application of organized military force, especially when such force is available, nowhere appears on the traditional halakhic agenda. Maimonides did not address the subject in his "Laws of Kings and their Wars"; and neither do any of his subsequent commentators.

Secularists interpret the silence of the available texts as an admission that the *halakhah* abdicates (and rightly so, in their view) all responsibility in matters which are properly the exclusive provenance of the democratically elected government.[43] Religiously committed Jews reject any such inference. Believing that every aspect of life, public as well as private, is amenable to definition in terms of traditional categories they instead look to their rabbinic guides to take up the challenge of peace with the same vigor once applied to war. More specifically, they expect rabbinic authorities to discover within the existing sources

---

[43] This view was articulated with particular vigour in the wake of the assassination of Prime Minister Rabin in November 1995. Individual rabbis were then summoned to police stations and required to explain some of the supposedly inflammatory rulings which they were reported to have issued against the peace process and its instigators. For rabbinic complaints, and for a re-iteration of the determination to continue to express religious opinions on matters of political substance, see the report of the biennial conference of Israeli rabbis in *Ha-Tzofeh* (the daily newspaper published by the MAFDAL), 18 February 1996.

allusions which, however tangentially, can in fact be thought to apply to present circumstances.

The response to that summons has been overwhelming. Since the early 1990s, the rabbinic community in its various shades and forms has produced a particularly rich and varied diet of scholarly analyses and public pronouncements, oral and written, all designed to express *Torah*-true opinion on the peace process and its progress. Much of the material is couched in the arcane lingua franca of traditional talmudic discourse, and hence intelligible only to relatively small coteries of cognoscenti. Nevertheless, once the several layers of scholasticism are peeled away, two antagonistic views can clearly be discerned and briefly summarized. One school of contemporary rabbinic thought denies the government a right to forego Israeli rule over the territories. The other, by contrast, invests the government with a prerogative to come to any such decision if advised to do so by the military authorities.

The concluding section of this chapter does not seek to encompass every detail of that debate. Still less will it attempt to weigh the relative merits of the proof texts mobilized by the two sides. Its purpose, rather, is simply to provide some illustrations of the arguments which each has adduced in support of its own particular case.

VI

At root, national-religious opposition to the pace and direction of the peace process derives from the understanding that no human government possesses the right to contravene a Divine commandment. In "Laws of Kings and their Wars" (III:9), Maimonides ruled that "should the king come to nullify the word of the *Torah*, he is not to be obeyed." This maxim, it is argued, clearly applies to any government attempt to relinquish Jewish sovereignty over the Holy Land. After all, the entire world is the Lord's, and it was He who apportioned the Land of Israel to Abraham, Isaac, Jacob and their descendants as an everlasting inheritance. That privilege necessarily entails various obligations. One, originally formulated by Rabbi Moses ben Nahman, (Nachmanides 1194–1270) as an addendum to the Maimonidean code, and at an early stage of Zionist history elevated to a central tenet of national-religious belief, is the binding duty to settle in the Holy Land. Another, posited with particular emphasis after 1967, is that Israel's possession of its patrimony can never be voluntarily renounced. As one rabbinic opponent of the Oslo accords put it:

"None of us owns the Land of Israel. Hence, none of us has any right to relinquish any portion of the entire country."[44]

That relatively simplistic appeal to transcendental imperatives has of late been complemented by a somewhat more sophisticated framework of analysis. Indeed, and as several observers have noted, rabbinic opposition to the Oslo agreement has shifted its ground. Whereas it at one time displayed an axiomatic preoccupation with the metaphysical properties of the Land of Israel, it now focuses far more explicitly on the tangibles of national defence.[45] Just how far the pivot of polemic had thus moved was illustrated in a pronouncement which a group of over 200 Israeli rabbis first published late in 1993, and which was reprinted as a privately-funded advertisement, in both the national religious Israeli daily newspaper, *Ha-Tzofeh*, on 15 December 1995 and (much more incongruously) in the avowedly secularist *Ha-Aretz* daily as recently as 5 March, 1996. The inherent sanctity of Judea and Samaria, this group claimed,

---

[44] Rabbi Mordechai Eliyahu (former Sephardi Chief Rabbi of Israel), *Ha-Tzofeh*, 14 Sept. 1993. For an earlier, and by now classic, exposition of the first theme: see Rabbi Mosheh Zvi Neriyah, "Our Right to the Land of Israel" (1974), cited in Shaviv, op. cit., pp. 30–33. Much of the argumentation is conveniently summarized in English in: Rav Nachum Eliezer Rabinovitch, "Conquest of the Land of Israel According to the Ramban" and "Possession of the Land of Israel", *Crossroads*, 2 (1988), pp. 181–205.

[45] Aryeh Naor, "The National-Religious ('Credo') Argument against the Israel-PLO Accord: A Worldview Tested by Reality" (Hebrew), *State and Religion Yearbook 1993*, pp. 54–88.

constitutes only one dimension of the case against any reduction in the IDF's control over those territories. The same argument is further buttressed by security considerations — of which the most relevant, certainly in religious terms, is the overriding need to avoid endangering Jewish lives and thereby transgressing the admonition contained in Leviticus 19:16 "Thou shalt not stand aside while the blood of thy neighbour is being shed".

Significantly, the required proof text for this argument does not appear in Maimonides' discussion of "Kings and their Wars". Instead, it is tucked away in his review of the complex do's and don'ts of sabbath observance. There, its specific context is the resolution of the dilemma which could arise were the prohibition against handling weapons on the sabbath to conflict with the obligation to save Jewish life [*pikuah nefesh*]. Once again, the Maimonidean decision, itself based on talmudic precedents and endorsed by all subsequent rabbinic authorities,[46] is absolutely clear.

"If Israelite cities are besieged by heathens, the rule is as follows: If the heathens have come because of a dispute over money, the Sabbath may not be violated on their account, nor may war be waged against them, unless the city is situated close to the borders of the Land of Israel, for in that case one may sally forth armed with weapons and may violate the sabbath on their account, even if they have come because of a dispute over stubble and straw.[47] If, however, the heathens have come to take life, or are preparing for battle, or if the motive for the siege is unknown, then wherever the city may be situated, one may sally forth armed with weapons and violate the Sabbath on their account.

Furthermore, it is a religious duty [*mitzvah*] for all Israelites who are able to do so, to come and sally forth on the Sabbath to assist their besieged brethren and to deliver them from the heathens; indeed, it is forbidden to postpone doing so until after the Sabbath. Having delivered their brethren, they are likewise permitted to return home with their weapons on the Sabbath, in order that they should not be tempted to stay away on a future occasion."[48]

---

[46] In fact, the authority cited by the signatories to the advertisement in *Ha-Tzofeh* was the 16th century compendium, known as the *Shulhan Arukh*: "Orah Hayyim", Sabbath Laws, 329:6. The language (and the ruling) in this source repeat Maimonides.

[47] An allusion to the Philistine attack on the village of Kielah; see I Sam. 23:1 as interpreted in BT *Eruvin*, folio 56a.

[48] *The Book of Seasons*, "The Sabbath", 2:23. *The Code of Maimonides*, Book 3 (trans. by S. Gandz & H. Klein; New Haven: Yale University Press, 1961), p. 17.

VII

Whether or not this ruling has any relevance to the present situation in Israel occasions a great deal of learned scrutiny. Rabbinic scholars opposed to the current peace process answer very definitely in the affirmative. Jewish settlements on the West Bank, they argue, unquestionably qualify as "border settlements". Hence, their inhabitants have a religious obligation to take up arms — even on the sabbath and even in defence of their property.[49] What is more, "all Israelites who are able to do so" (and surely none are better equipped than IDF troops) must likewise participate in their defence. Indeed, if some of the earliest commentators on the traditional codes are to be followed, they must mobilize even before the threat actually materializes, in order to maintain what contemporary strategists refer to as a credible posture of deterrence.[50] In short, the situation under review constitutes a clear instance of *pikuah nefesh* and must be categorized as an obligatory war (*milkhemet mitzvah*). That being so, the government possesses no authority whatsoever to exercise discretion in its conduct. A resort to arms is mandatory.

Proponents of an alternative school of rabbinic thought reject any such inference. In the most interesting of instances, they do so by likewise appealing to the bar of traditional halakhic precedent. Not for them, therefore, the contention that ex cathedra rabbinic rulings possess no authoritative status in a democratic system of government — a contention which, however valid in some eyes, most religious circles find discomforting. Instead, they resort to the time-honoured rules and referents of traditional Jewish legal discourse in order to make an entirely different point. Indeed, basic to the conclusions posited by this school

---

[49] Rabbi Ya'akov Ariel, "Self-Defence (the *intifadah* in the *halakhah*)" (Hebrew), *Tehumin*, 10 (1989), pp. 62–75.

[50] Thus, in his authoritative gloss to the *Shulhan Arukh*, Rabbi Moses Isserlis (1525–1572) ruled that the commandment applies: "Even if they [the Gentiles] have not yet attacked but merely demonstrate a willingness to do so".

of thought is the argument that, on strictly theological grounds, rabbinic judgments must follow the guidance provided by non-rabbinic specialists, who possess the competence to decide on matters requiring military expertise.

An essay entitled "Ceding Territory of the Land of Israel in Order to Save Lives" provides a conspicuous example of the latter genre.[51] Although published in 1990 (and hence written before the current peace process gathered momentum), the essay remains a landmark in the intra-rabbinic debate. One reason for that reputation is the continued relevance of its content. Another, almost equally as apposite in the rabbinic world, is the towering prestige of its author, Rabbi Ovadiah Yosef, a former Sephardi Chief Rabbi of Israel, and a man widely regarded as one of the most pre-eminent of all living halakhic authorities [*poskei halakhah*].

In the very first sentence of his essay, Rabbi Ovadiah Yosef disclaims any intention of delivering "a halakhic ruling whether the government of Israel should return territories of the Land of Israel or not." What he presents, instead, is a rabbinic commission, which authorizes the government to reach its own decision, quite independently of religious pressure one way or another. Coming from a rabbi, that is a radical position, but one which (so he claims) traditional rabbinic methodology can comfortably accommodate. After all, for centuries rabbis have deferred to doctors (including, he adds, non-Jewish doctors) when deciding whether or not a sick person may eat or drink on the Day of Atonement, which under any other circumstances is a mortal sin. In so doing, they have not divested themselves of their own authority to decide which path to follow. On the contrary, they have given the full force of halakhic backing to medical advice. Precisely the same procedure must be followed

---

[51] Rav Ovadiah Yosef, "Ceding Territory of the Land of Israel in Order to Save Lives", *Crossroads*, 3 (1990), pp. 11–28. For an astute legal-philosophical analysis of the text see: Yitzchak Engelhard, "The Halakhic Problem of Ceding Territories of the Land of Israel: Law and Ideology" (Hebrew), *Ha-Praklit*, 13 (1993), pp. 13–34.

when deciding on matters of national security. Here, too, *halakhah* does not relinquish all responsibility. Instead, it explicitly requires that non-halakhic "expert opinion" has the last word.

In this view, the appropriate point of departure is neither the inherent sanctity of the Land of Israel nor even the deterrent value which might attach to the defence of "border settlements". Even if the *halakhah* accepts both propositions (Rabbi Ovadiah Yosef himself emphatically concurs with the first but questions the second), its exponents cannot adduce either as a basis for deciding whether military activity is to be pursued or suspended. The only acceptable touchstone of judgement is the principle of *pikuah nefesh* and the degree to which a particular course of action promises to save, or endanger, the greatest number of human lives. Thus approached, the definition of a *milkhemet reshut* as a "discretionary" or "licensed" war is given a novel twist and an added dimension. The power of discretion is not limited solely to the members of the "court of 71". It is also vested in the military experts responsible for evaluating the prospects of operational success. Indeed, the need to subscribe to their opinions constitutes a binding halakhic instruction.

"If the commanders of the army, together with the political experts, determine that retaining the territories entails *pikuah nefesh*, we rely on their judgement and permit the cessation of territory." (p. 18).

To adopt any other course is to run the risk of causing unnecessary death.

VIII

For all his eminence, Rabbi Ovadiah Yosef's opinion has not met with universal approval. Thus, the polemic continues.[52] Given the tendency of rabbinic discourse to think in time-spans

[52] Compare the response which the editors of *Crossroads* (in what appears to be a deliberate effort to maintain their own impartiality) published in the same issue of the journal. Rav Shaul Yisraeli, "Ceding Territory Because of Mortal Danger",

which are measured by centuries, it is likely to do so for some time to come. Meanwhile, however, the "battle of books" has already injected an almost unprecedented tone of vehemence and invective into the rhetoric of all public discussions on security affairs. This situation not only provokes discord and disarray within the religious community *per se*. At one remove, it also impinges on relationships between religious and secular segments of Israeli society at large, generating disputes over one of the few topics which — because related to national defence — was traditionally considered immune to contentious exchange. By the standards of past Israeli experience, this shift in style amounts to a change of truly momentous proportions. Issues of war and peace, once debated in a prevailing spirit of compatible empiricism, and with a wide measure of agreement about fundamental national priorities, now have to bear the encumbrance of rival ideologies and conflicting religious interpretations. It is to a review of how that situation intersects with other religious tensions within the ranks of the IDF that attention must now be turned.

---

ibid., pp. 29–46. Still more elaborate, and outspoken, is Eliav Shochatman, *And He Confirmed it to Jacob as a Statute: On the Validity of the People of Israel's Sovereignty Over the Land of Israel and on the Question of our Retention of the Land of Israel With and Without Danger to Life* (Hebrew; Jerusalem: Karta, 1995). Compare: Rabbi Amnon Bazak, *"And Thou Shalt Live By Them": An Enquiry into the Question of the Sanctity of Life and the Integrity of the Land* (Hebrew: Jerusalem: Meimad, 1993).

TWO

From Integration to Segregation: The Role of Religion in the IDF

The role played by religion in Israeli military service is inherently complex. So much is this so that it resists classification in accordance with the paradigms conventionally employed by political analysts. True, the IDF does at first glance appear to be the military instrument of a secular and liberal state, in which religious objectives are not adduced as overt justifications for the shedding of blood. In that sense, the relationship between religion and military service in Israel is clearly distinct from the nexus forged throughout history by the armed forces of theocratic regimes, a category which embraces examples otherwise as dissimilar as the knightly orders of medieval Christendom and the Islamic fundamentalist guards of contemporary Iran. On the other hand, however, neither does the IDF conform to the rigidly secular model of modern, western military organizations, in which spiritual themes are confined to the severely restricted demesne allowed to the army chaplain. Indeed, all attempts to dragoon the IDF into any such mould are precluded by the ubiquity with which explicitly religious motifs permeate the IDF's ethos and are frequently, sometimes blatantly, mobilized for military purposes.

When confronted with cases which defy conventional categorization, social scientists often attempt to posit an entirely new methodological framework, hoping thereby to reconcile the contradictions which they observe. The purposes of the present chapter are more modest. Discussion will initially be confined to a delineation of the various roles which religion plays in Israeli military service. Only thereafter will attention be focused on an examination of the pressures to which the relationship thus established is presently being subjected.

I

Crucial to an understanding of all aspects of military life in Israel, and not least to an appreciation of the relationship between religion and military service, is the fact that the IDF has always projected and protected its image as a "people's army".[1] Of the several connotations associated with that designation, two are generally considered salient. One concerns the diverse nature of tasks which the Force performs; the other appertains more directly to the varied backgrounds from which its personnel are recruited. At root, both of these attributes stem from a common impulse, broadly identified as a determination to convert the military into an instrument of social engineering. Nevertheless, since their expressions and implications remain distinct, each warrants independent description.

Many of the tasks undertaken by the IDF come under the rubric of what contemporary military jargon labels "missions other than war" (MOTW). This is another way of saying that the activities assigned to the armed forces are not restricted to fighting foreign or domestic foes. Rather, they also extend to the performance of public service functions whose implementation makes no particular demands on specifically combat-related skills. Notwithstanding the persistence and range of its conventional security burdens, the IDF has traditionally devoted a large proportion of its corporate energies to non-violent missions, acting as an agency for the realization of projects with high civilian content. Indeed, its institutional posture offers a prototype of benign "military role expansion" — the process whereby armed forces tailor their military networks to meet civilian needs and:

---

[1] For an illustration of the extent to which the IDF prides itself on that image see: Louis Williams, *Israel Defense Force: A People's Army* (Tel- Aviv: Ministry of Defense Publications, 1989).

"... thus penetrate into various institutional fields, such as economic enterprises, education and training of civilian manpower, fulfilling civilian administrative functions"[2]

In many other developing states, the phenomenon of "military role expansion" reflects crudely organizational constraints. Quite simply, the armed forces constitute the only framework in possession of the human and material resources required in order to construct the infrastructure of roads, factories and schools which new nations aspire to put on the map. In Israel's case, however, such considerations have been supplemented by ideological motives. The IDF serves as an instrument for the attainment of national goals which are as much symbolic as they are material. Thus employed, the military apparatus promulgates the most fundamental of the values to which all (Jewish) citizens subscribe, whatever their political affiliations or degree of adherence to the precepts of traditional religious observance. One paradigmatic example is provided by the NAHAL [Youth Pioneer Fighting] Corps, set up in 1949 in order to facilitate the foundation of communes (*kibbutzim*) in areas considered too remote or insecure for civilian habitation, and thus to express the Zionist ethos of land settlement (*hityashvut*). Another is the establishment within the Education Corps of a special subsection, mandated to provide supplementary instruction for schoolchildren and new recruits in under-privileged communities, and thus to exemplify the national commitment to equality of opportunity. Yet a third consists of the provisions made (especially during the 1950s) to enlist IDF engineering and medical units in the task of immigrant absorption and thus to ensure the success of *aliyah* (Jewish immigration), a commitment itself enshrined in Israel's Declaration of Independence.[3]

---

[2] Moshe Lissak, *Military Roles in Modernization* (Beverly Hills, Ca: Sage,1976), p. 13.

[3] Thomas Bowden, *Army in The Service of the State* (Tel-Aviv: University Publishing Projects, 1976); Daniella Ashkenazy (ed.), *The Military in the Service of Society and Democracy: The Challenge of the Dual-Role Military* (Westport: Greenwood Press, 1994).

The contribution which the varied nature of the IDF's assignments made to its image as a "people's army" has been further reinforced, secondly, by the singularity of its force structure. Military service in Israel has never been restricted to those citizens who elect to make the armed forces their career. With the significant — but nevertheless singular — exception of Muslim Arabs, neither has enlistment been discriminatory. Rather, Israel has ever since 1948 adhered to the rule of compulsory and universal conscription. All youngsters, female as well as male, are drafted into the IDF when they reach the age of 18 for terms of, respectively, 21 and 36 months. Furthermore, reservists (for the most part males) are also liable for additional terms of one month's duty per annum until middle age.[4] Ever coy about divulging manpower statistics, Israel's military authorities provide no precise figures of the troops which this unique system of national service places under arms. Nevertheless, the general picture is clear. As portrayed by the International Institute for Strategic Studies, the IDF resembles a three-tiered pyramid. Its base consists of the mass of reservists (estimated to number some 430,000 trained troops available for immediate summons); conscripts (about 140,000) comprise its central backbone; and a small cadre of long-service and professional regulars (circa 35,000) form its apex.[5] This structure ensures that the burdens of military duty are fairly evenly spread throughout society. It also accounts for the fact that service in the ranks has become the most widely-shared of national experiences and the single most formative experience in the life of the vast majority of individual citizens.[6] As a "people's army", the IDF is thus not only a Force which serves the entire nation; it likewise incor-

---

[4] For details of the relevant legislation, see: Edward Luttwak and Dan Horowitz, *The Israeli Army* (New York: Harper & Row, 1975), pp. 85–98, 424–6.

[5] *The Military Balance, 1995–1996* (London; Brassey's, 1995), p. 136.

[6] Ofra Mayseless, "Military Service as a Central Feature of the Israeli Experience" (Hebrew), *Sekirah Hodshit* (IDF monthly; issued to all officers), 40 (January 1993), pp. 3–6.

porates the major portion of the citizen-body of which the nation is composed.

Our present context does not require an elaboration of the strategic considerations thought to justify the IDF's preference for what is essentially a militia system. It is sufficient merely to recite the conventional wisdom: a force structure dependant on compulsory conscripts and reservists was (and to some extent still is) considered the most efficient method whereby Israel might compensate for her inherent demographic inferiority vis-a-vis her potential foes and maintain a constant state of military preparedness, without either disrupting her economic well-being or endangering her political equilibrium.[7] Far more relevant to the themes of this book are the social stimulants which generated the choice of that particular system of recruitment. These were stressed with particular vigour by David Ben-Gurion (1886–1973), Israel's first prime minister and minister of defence (he held both positions between 1948 and 1953 and from 1955 until 1963), and the man chiefly responsible for creating the IDF and defining its character. From the very first, Ben-Gurion intended the military to become an instrument of new Jewish "nation building" and a symbolic focus of national sentiment. Above all, he envisioned the IDF as a bonding institution within which Israel's otherwise fractured society could be homogenized and welded into a single whole. In his own words, addressed to a group of newly inducted officers as early as 1949:

"While the first mission of the IDF ... is the security of the State, that is not its only task. The Army must also serve as a pioneering educational force for Israeli youth, both native-born and immigrants. The IDF must educate a pioneering generation, healthy in body and spirit, brave and faithful, which will heal tribal and Diaspora

---

[7] The received wisdom is detailed in Baruch Kimmerling, *The Interrupted System: Israeli Civilians in War and Routine Times* (New Brunswick, N. J. : Transaction Books, 1985). For current reservations, see: Emanuel Wald, *The Gordion Knot: Myths and Dilemmas of Israeli National Security* (Hebrew: Yediot Aharonot; Tel-Aviv, 1992), pp. 166–71 and Shemuel Gordon, "In Favour of Selective Conscription" (Hebrew), *Ma'archot*, 328 (February 1993), pp. 32–37.

divisions and implement the historic missions of the State of Israel through a process of self-fulfillment, by building the homeland and making its deserts bloom."[8]

II

Ben-Gurion's credo impinged upon the relationship between religion and military service in Israel in at least three crucial respects. First, by mandating universal military conscription, it explicitly rejected the notion that religious and secular citizens possessed different sets of civic obligations. The patriotic duty, indeed right, of military service was equally incumbent on members of both communities. Second, the same principle of equity also precluded religious troops from serving in their own distinctive military formations. To allow them to do so (or, for that matter, to compel them to do so) would merely emphasize their singularity and thereby undermine the goal of national integration which the IDF was designed to fulfil. However, by the same token — and thirdly — the military had clearly also to accommodate itself to the particular needs of religious personnel. Thus, the entire IDF framework had to be structured in ways which would not alienate religiously observant troops by requiring them to contravene the dictates of traditional Jewish law.

The organizational requirements imposed by this tripartite cluster of considerations became apparent even before the IDF was officially established. Indeed, they generated a lengthy series of debates, which continued to occupy the attention of the General Staff throughout Israel's War of Independence in 1948–9. At a distance of half a century, many of the issues involved seem somewhat petty; most merit definition as little more than institutional tussles over bureaucratic turf between different branches of the fledgling military apparatus. What is

---

[8] David Ben-Gurion, *Uniqueness and Mission* (Hebrew; Tel-Aviv: Am-Oved, 1971), p. 81. In general: Yoav Gelber, "Ben-Gurion and the Creation of the IDF", *Jerusalem Quarterly*, 50 (1990), pp. 83–5.

more, several of the more bitter intra-military controversies (all
laboriously exhumed from the archives in Dr. Zahava Ostfeld's
massive study of the re-organization of Jewish fighting power
in the years 1947–1949[9]), were occasioned by only minor
infractions of military discipline — in one instance on the part
of two cooks who refused to prepare a hot meal on the sabbath.[10]
Beneath this apparently trivial surface, however, there lurked
a range of fundamental concerns, none of which was belied
by the fact that religiously observant troops at this early stage
usually amounted to only ten per cent of the total fighting
complement. As all parties to the debate fully appreciated, none
more so than Ben-Gurion, at stake was nothing less than the
future character of the embryonic Force and the locus of its
ultimate source of authority.

Both before and immediately after the establishment of the
IDF, representatives of the national religious political parties
claimed that the interests of their constituents in uniform required two organizational steps. One was the establishment of
a military chaplaincy, endowed with much wider powers than
the existing "religious service" section of the Manpower Branch;
the other was the continued enlistment of religious troops into
homogeneous units of their own, such as had already been
formed under the auspices of the *Haganah* (the largest of the
pre-State Jewish "underground" organizations). Ben-Gurion enthusiastically endorsed the first suggestion; but emphatically
rejected the second. In both instances, he justified his response
by reference to his wider vision of the implications involved.
His own ambition, he argued on several occasions, was to inculcate
basic Jewish values into the IDF in its entirety, and thus to

---

[9] Zahava Ostfeld, *An Army is Born: Main Stages in the Buildup of the Army under
the Leadership of David Ben-Gurion* (Hebrew; 2 vols: Tel-Aviv, Ministry of Defense
Publications, 1994), esp. pp. 439–441 and 746–751.

[10] In his personal diary, Ben-Gurion himself referred to this single incident on three
separate occasions in September 1948, a time when he might have reasonably been
excused for thinking that events at the front deserved his undivided attention. Ostfeld,
p. 748.

endow the Force with the humanistic ethos which he considered to be Judaism's greatest contribution to civilization. A military rabbinate could facilitate that aim, and should therefore be encouraged to concern itself with education in the broadest sense (his own, deliberately secular, term was "culture") and not merely with the details of religious practice. Precisely the same impulse, on the other hand, invalidated the need for distinct religious units. Their establishment would merely transfer into the military framework the secular-religious divisions which were already threatening to undermine the cohesion of Israeli society at large. His instructions were therefore as emphatic as they were terse. "Our army will be a united army, without 'trends'".[11]

On the grounds that a single, united and sovereign state required the maintenance of a unified military organization, Ben-Gurion had already insisted on the disestablishment (if necessary by force) of all the separate militias established prior to the declaration of Israel's independence by rival political parties. To that end, not only did he incorporate the *Haganah* into the IDF and disband the *Etzel* [*Irgun Tzeva'i Leumi*] and *Lehi* [*Lohamei Herut Yisrael*], the two smaller underground formations established by Revisionists and by the "Stern gang" respectively, in 1931 and in 1940.[12] In what is generally considered a supreme act of early statesmanship, he also demolished the autonomy of the *Palmach* (the *Haganah*'s elite striking force, closely identified with the Achdut Ha-Avodah Party), most dramatically by dismissing its high command.[13] Ben-Gurion saw no reason whatsoever why religious affiliations should constitute grounds for a departure from the standard of military uniformity thus imposed. In fact he altogether allowed

---

[11] Ostfeld, p. 749.

[12] In general, Ostfeld, pp. 599–741. For a more detailed study see, Joseph Heller, *The Stern Gang* (London: Frank Cass, 1995).

[13] Anita Shapira, *The Army Controversy, 1948* (Hebrew; Tel-Aviv: Ha-Kibbutz Ha-Meuchad, 1985).

only two exceptions to the IDF's adherence to an integrated force structure, and both were marginal. One applied to conscripts drawn from the tiny Druze minority, long time allies of the Jewish community in Palestine, whose ethnic and cultural distinctiveness justified their conscription into small units of their own.[14] The other concerned volunteers to the NAHAL corps, who were permitted to form homogenous "nuclei" (*garinim*) prior to enlistment, and were then drafted *en bloc*.[15] But no such arrangements could be extended to religious conscripts.

"I fear that the creation of religious units will result in the creation of anti-religious units.... It is preferable, and possible, to educate officers and commanders to understand and respect the religious soldier."[16]

III

Resilience is perhaps the most striking feature of the groundrules laid down by Ben-Gurion. True, the IDF top brass dragged its feet somewhat before constructing the institutional apparatus required in order to facilitate the full integration of religious and secular troops within a single framework. Not until late in 1949, for instance, was the IDF rabbinate (*ha-rabbanut ha-tzeva'it*) relieved of its subordination to the Manpower Branch, and its commander, the army Chief Rabbi (*ha-rav ha-tzeva'i ha-rashi*), awarded the rank of major-general with an *ex officio* seat on the General Staff. Even then, individual spokesmen for religious interests complained about the deficiencies of this body, and hence occasionally continued to advocate separate draft regulations for religious and secular recruits. In time, however, most such objections were easily brushed aside. "Integration" attained the status of an article of military faith; as such, it

---

[14] David Coren, *Steadfast Alliance: The Druze Community in Palestine and the Haganah* (Hebrew; Tel-Aviv: Ministry of Defense Publications, 1991).

[15] Yair Doar, *Ours is the Sickle and the Sword* (Hebrew; Efal: Yad Tabenkin, 1992).

[16] Reply to the Mizrachi (religious) party, 23 September 1949; cited in Ostfeld, p. 441.

constituted a yardstick by which all other considerations had to be measured. In practical terms, the result was a working compromise. The military establishment accommodated itself to the organizational constraints of an army rabbinate, composed of personnel whose primary ties of professional allegiance extended beyond the narrow confines of the military framework. On the other hand, the *rabbanut tzeva'it* adapted itself to addressing the needs of the entire military organization, and not those of just a small percentage of the overall complement.

The pattern thus laid down has persisted from Ben-Gurion's day until our own. Religion does not exist as a segmented "sub-culture" within the wider Israeli military fabric. Rather, it constitutes one of the IDF's integral components. Within the Force, traditional Jewish rituals, symbols and practices intrude on life in a multiplicity of spheres and at various levels. Hence, only in part do they cater to the specific requirements of those troops who profess orthodox Jewish beliefs. More extensively, they act as integrative referents for the IDF as a whole. By so doing, they generate a symbiosis between religion and military service in Israel which, even if not altogether unique in military history, is certainly more pervasive than that experienced in other modern and western armed forces.

One measure of that symbiosis is supplied by a closer examination of the structure and jurisdiction of the IDF rabbinate. In neither sphere does the *rabbanut ha-tzeva'it* suffer from the limitations which a general climate of secularism invariably imposes on chaplaincies in other western armies. On the contrary, its size and powers have increased out of all proportion to the growth of the IDF as a whole. What was originally a skeleton apparatus, directed merely "to advise the Chief of Staff on religious affairs", has expanded into a full-blown military formation which, in the words of one official IDF publication, is now:

"fully integrated into the army down to the battalion level and represented in every unit by a religious affairs officer or a religious affairs coordinator who attend to the religious needs of the unit and its soldiers."[17]

From a bureaucratic perspective, the most obtrusive symptom of this development has been the expansion in the size of the Rabbinate's complement, which now runs to several hundred troops and encompasses a full range of ranks, including three full colonels. But to this must be added other signs of institutional health. The *rabbanut tzeva'it* also possesses its own distinctive unit emblem (the two stone tablets of the ten commandments upheld by a sword) and its own tradition of battlefield valour (supplied by the exemplary service performed under fire by members of the *hevra kadisha* branch, whose task is to identify fatal casualties and bring them to burial). Under the aegis of its three successive commanders and their numerous assistants, it has also developed its own training programme; its own choir and entertainment troupe (first formed in 1963); its own in-house publication (*Machanayim*; literally "camps", a play on Genesis 32:3);[18] its own military tribunal; and — always a sure sign of status in the military pecking-order — its own headquarters compound.

Many of the duties performed by this extensive workforce are certainly sectoral, in the sense that they cater for needs which only professing religious troops might regularly require. The provision of spiritual guidance and counsel, for instance, is the duty of officers serving in the IDF rabbinate, several of whom are qualified rabbis. Other ranks are responsible for the

---

[17] IDF Spokesman, Information Branch, Publication No. 22/93, "IDF Military Rabbinate" (July 1993), pp. 1–2. The only account of the development of the IDF Rabbinate is Benny Michaelson, "Ha-Rabbanut ha-Tzeva'it", in: *The IDF and its Arms*, vol. 16 (Hebrew: eds. I. Kfir and Y. Erez; Tel-Aviv: Revivim, 1982), pp. 83–132.

[18] For a survey of the contents of this publication, which appeared on a weekly basis for most of the 1950s and 1960s (when it was also billed as "a synagogue journal for the soldier") and more sporadically thereafter: Akiva Zimmerman, "Machanayim — The Story of a Religious Military Journal" (Hebrew), *Kesher*, 12 (November 1992), pp. 108–115.

upkeep of a synagogue on every military installation, and for the maintenance of a regular supply of the manifold ritual artifacts (phylacteries, prayer shawls, prayer books) which practicing orthodox Jews require on a daily basis. That bald catalogue of commissions, however, belies the extent of influence which the *rabbanut ha-tzeva'it* effectively wields. General Staff regulations invest the rabbinate with a mandate designed to ensure that army life in its entirety conforms to some of the most rigorous precepts of traditional Jewish law. Moreover, the compendia of religious rulings which the *rav tzeva'i rashi* publishes from time to time possess military authority and are incorporated into the overall military code. He alone has the right to decide when a serviceman declared "missing in action" might be assumed dead (and whether, therefore, his wife might re-marry under Jewish law). Similarly, in the extraordinary circumstances encountered when an immigrant's religious status is in doubt, the IDF Chief Rabbi and his tribunal have also been granted the prerogative to sanction an enlisted soldier's conversion to Judaism.[19]

Thus to note the degree of role expansion permitted to the *rabbanut tzeva'it* is not to suggest that most Israeli military personnel subscribe to orthodox Jewish beliefs or observe traditional religious practices. Here, too, the IDF itself provides no precise data; but it can reasonably be assumed that no more than 12–15% of the overall complement of regulars, conscripts and reservists come from religious homes and rely upon the chaplaincy to ensure that IDF practice conforms to the dictates of their consciences. The reason why the self-confessedly secular majority nevertheless accepts the impositions (and is prepared to suffer the personal inconveniences) imposed by traditional Jewish law lie elsewhere. Basically, it responds to two impulses. One is a readiness to respect the beliefs of the religious minority; another, is an acknowledgement of the need to create and sustain the environment which orthodox troops require in

---

[19] Michaelson, "Ha-Rabbanut Ha-Tzeva'it", p. 97.

order to express their beliefs through the medium of ritual practice. Together, both considerations illustrate the degree to which integrative determinants permit the interests of a minority to wield a degree of influence which the dry statistics of demography would otherwise belie.

A particularly striking illustration of the steps taken by the Israeli armed forces to accommodate religious needs within an overall framework of military practice is provided by the chain of command which exists in every IDF kitchen. The example is not chosen entirely at random. As Napoleon is so frequently reported to have pointed out, all armies march on their stomachs and meals therefore play a prominent role in all military life. Equally conspicuous is the severity and detail with which traditional Judaism insists that dietary regulations be observed. Quite apart from setting strict boundaries on the types of foods which Jews may and may not eat, Jewish law (the *halakhah*) also mandates the rigorous separation of meat and dairy products and utensils. To complicate matters even further, supplementary dietary stipulations also apply during the week of Passover, when no leavened foods may be eaten and all crockery has to be changed or specially prepared. No observant Jew or Jewess would wish to serve in units in which this intricate bounty of regulations was not observed. And it is precisely in order to make it possible for them to do so — as equals — that officers and NCO's attached to the *rabbanut ha-tzeva'it* are appointed as "supervisors" (*mashgichim*) in every IDF mess and orchestrate an "Operation Passover" every spring. What is more, within the kitchen, final decisions rest with the "supervisor" rather than the mess orderly or even the unit commander.

Similar conditions apply with regard to sabbath observance. Here, too, the *halakhah* lays down a complex network of ordinances with respect to the categories of activities which are permitted and prohibited. Within the latter category come even such ostensibly non-laborious tasks as writing, switching on electricity, communicating by telephone, travelling in a vehicle, and carrying any item in the public domain. All such prohibitions must be transgressed when life is endangered. Hence, they do not preclude active defense in the face of attack. But where exactly is the line to be drawn? Does guard duty fall within the category of "saving life"? Do regular training exercises? For present purposes, the answer to those questions (yes in the case of the first, no in the second[20]) is less relevant than the identity of the authority empowered to deliver a decision. On this point, IDF regulations are both emphatic and explicit. Once again, the word of the *rabbanut ha-tzeva'it* and its local representatives on the spot is authoritative, overriding even the local unit commander.

IV

The extraordinary extent to which the IDF tolerates the subordination of narrowly-defined military considerations to orthodox Jewish requirements constitutes only one, bureaucratized, aspect of the relationship between religion and military service in Israel. Equally important is the role played by a still more extensive web of traditional Jewish symbols and themes. These do not appertain solely to the minutiae of orthodox religious practice, but draw on what (for want of a better term) can only be defined as the capacious mosaic of the Jewish heritage — that enormous legacy of shared associations, collective myths, and common means of expression which foster the retention of a specifically Jewish national identity. These arouse the sympathies of a constituency far larger than the avowedly orthodox segment of servicemen and women. In various ways, and for a variety of reasons, they strike responsive cords amongst the non-observant mass of personnel, many of whom define themselves as "traditionalists."[21] As a result, they play a particularly

---

[20] The two examples chosen are by far the simplest. For a detailed discussion of some of the knottier problems which frequently arise see: Rav Avraham Y. Neriya, "Shabbat Suspension in Cases of Danger in the Army", *Crossroads*, 4 (1991), pp. 249–262.

[21] The background and nuances of "traditionalism" amongst Israeli Jews are explored

crucial function in the process whereby the entire Force in welded into a cohesive whole.

In part, the *rabbanut ha-tzeva'it* itself supplies the agency through which specifically religious Jewish cultural symbols and themes are disseminated throughout the military framework. That, indeed, is the task expressly allotted to the "religious tradition and knowledge" branch of the IDF rabbinate, to which the General Staff allocates responsibility "for instilling Jewish values [and] stressing the destiny and distinction of the Jewish people in their own country".[22] Acting on this commission, the branch regularly conducts day-long seminars on Jewish ethics and history for individual cohorts of conscripts, who are also provided with occasional publications which summarize traditional religious teachings in a manner designed to make them intelligible to the uninitiated. Additional emphasis is placed on such topics in the IDF's Officer's Training School, where lectures and discussions on such themes as "The Army in Jewish Perspective" or "What is Judaism ?" constitute an integral part of the curriculum. Still more extensive, finally, is the IDF rabbinate's annual "Awakening Campaign", conducted every autumn during the month which precedes the Jewish New Year and Day of Atonement. Transformed into a regular fixture on the military calendar ever since 1959 (thereto it had been a voluntary matter, left to the discretion of individual commanders), the "Awakening Campaign" provides the IDF rabbinate with an opportunity to introduce troops to both the major ritual practices of the period and to some of the spiritual messages which such practices are meant to promulgate.[23]

How effective all this hustle and bustle might be must remain an open question. Interviewed in the winter of 1995–1996, most officers attached to the relevant branch of the *rabbanut*

---

in: Charles S. Liebman and Steven M. Cohen, *Two Worlds of Judaism: The Israeli and American Experiences* (New Haven: Yale University Press, 1990).

[22] "The Military Rabbinate", p. 1

[23] Liebman and Don-Yehiya, *Civil Religion in Israel*, pp. 179–180.

tzeva'it professed to a feeling that their activities had made a "substantial" contribution to fostering Jewish awareness amongst their audiences. Personal observation, however, suggests that the evidence might not be quite so conclusive. The fact that synagogues attendance on IDF bases during the High Holy Days is considerably larger than at other times, for instance, does not itself prove the success of the "Awakening Campaign"; after all, the same is true throughout the country. It is similarly difficult to verify claims that the programmes of lectures organized by the IDF rabbinate make a contribution of any note to Jewish self-awareness amongst the troops. Certainly, the programmes themselves are generally popular; but the reasons for their favourable reception might lie elsewhere than in their content. At one of the seminars which I attended, the vast majority of young participants, conforming to the practice of soldiers the world over, took the opportunity provided by the break in their training schedule to fall into a deep sleep. On awakening, very few picked up the pamphlets laid out on the tables for their edification; and who is to say how many of those who did so actually read the text, let alone took to heart its message?

An awareness of the flaws inherent in any programme of formal education probably explains why the IDF has never relied solely on the institutional apparatus provided by the *rabbanut tzeva'it* to mobilize the vast spectrum of cultural resources which Judaism provides. Rather, traditional Jewish themes and motifs have been more subtly — albeit no less sedulously — woven into the texture of the Force by a variety of supplementary mechanisms, some of which are virtually subliminal. One is linguistic: the use of biblical Hebrew terminology to connote military ranks, humdrum commands and even home-produced battle platforms such as the "Kefir" [young lion] jet fighter and the "Merkavah" [chariot] tank. But others are more obviously ritual. For instance, while on active service, every member of the IDF, whatever his or her rank and military profession, is duty-bound to attend the ceremony of blessing the wine (*kiddush*) which precedes the Friday evening meal and marks the inauguration of the Sabbath. (It is indicative of the military aura attached to this rite that the blessing itself is invariably recited by the local CO, and not by a member of the *rabbanut tzeva'it*). Similarly, all Jewish military burials are performed in accordance with traditional religious practice. Moreover, although army rabbis and cantors are in attendance, the funeral oration itself is traditionally delivered by a senior officer.

The purposes which such intrusions of traditional Jewish practice serve clearly extend beyond the desire to harmonize the particularist concerns of the religious few with the more general interests of the non-religious many. Rather, they are designed to infuse the IDF as a whole with a sense of shared identity, shared values and shared purpose. This aim is particularly transparent during the week which marks the Hebrew anniversary of the outbreak of the Yom Kippur War in 1973. Ever since, the editors of *Ba-Mahaneh* ("In Camp"), the IDF's most popular weekly, have emphasized the symbolism inherent in the fact that the most severe of modern Israel's military trials commenced on the date which Jewish tradition reveres as the "Day of Judgement". Repeatedly stressed, accordingly, are such motifs as the common fate of Jewry and the function of faith as a stimulant to heroism under fire. Profusely illustrated, and produced in a glossy format, each annual issue of *Ba-Mahaneh* provides a striking demonstration (and regular reminder) of the extent to which the IDF transmits essentially religious themes to an overwhelmingly secular audience, thereby transmuting Judaism into an "integrative" military asset.[24] Traditional religious associations, at this level, serve as a social coagulant,

---

[24] Thus, the front cover of the 1995 "Yom Kippur" issue, dated 29 Sept. 1995, consists of a photograph of a prayer book and prayer shawl against a background of a military uniform and army name-tag. Of the 24 feature articles, four focus on personal memories of the 1973 war; three consist of discussions on the contemporary meaning of the Day of Atonement; two are photo-reports of various Jewish festival rites; three are short stories on set against a background of religious observance; one

and thus as a vehicle for fostering the feelings of affinity and reciprocity which have always been recognized to constitute essential criteria for military cohesion, and ultimately for effective battlefield performance.[25]

Every military organization known to history has exploited pageant for precisely the same purpose, and the IDF is no exception. What remains remarkable, nevertheless, is the extent to which each major rite of passage in the Israeli military experience is suffused with ceremonies which arouse profound Jewish connotations, and indeed are deliberately designed to do so. Once again, only the most striking examples need be cited. At his and her induction, every new recruit receives a copy of the Bible — which religious conscripts necessarily consider to be a sacred work and which secular troops, too, have been taught at school to regard as the most formative text in the entire Jewish literary corpus.[26] Similarly evocative are the venues frequently selected for the staging of passing-out parades. On completion of basic training, for instance, each new cohort of paratroops is formally enrolled in Jerusalem by torch-light at the western wall. The site is well-chosen. Quite apart from being the sole remaining relic of the second temple destroyed in the year 70 ce, and hence a place of religious pilgrimage, the western wall is also located at the heart of the Old City which the paratroop brigade "liberated" (to use common Israeli parlance) in a blaze of glory during the Six Days' War of 1967. In other infantry brigades similar ceremonies take place on the heights of Massada, the last bastion of resistance to Roman rule during the Jewish rebellion of 66–70 ce.

---

compares Jewish fast days with those observed in other religions; and another surveys the mystical teachings of a hasidic leader.

[25] This point is stressed and illustrated from a wide variety of contexts in: Richard Holmes, *Acts of War: The Behavior of Men in Battle* (New York: The Free Press, 1985), especially chapter 2: "Mysterious Fraternity".

[26] See, however, below, pp. 56–57.

VI

As recently as the early 1980s, analyses of the role of religion in Israeli military service could reasonably have broken off at this juncture and concluded on a generally affirmative note. Their perorations would almost certainly have been celebratory in tone. They could have included a short description of the way in which traditional Jewish values inject an ethical code of conduct into the IDF's corporate behaviour, thereby moderating the brutalizing influences which military frameworks, by the nature of their purposes, often exert.[27] Still more emphatically, they could — and did — depict the general relationship between religion and military duty in Israel in terms intended to suggest an overall picture of harmony. Common service was said to mitigate the stresses otherwise generated by intra-Jewish religious dissension in Israel, enabling both orthodox and secular segments of Jewish society to sublimate their separate interests within a military setting which tightens their communal bonds. As a "people's army", wrote Samuel Rolbant in 1970, the IDF

"has helped to break all barriers between men who lived all their lives in vastly different cultural milieus. Boys from religious families could mix freely with antireligious boys from secularist left-wing kibbutzim, learning to give and take, to disagree while respecting the other's right to his own view, to refrain from excesses of behavior and find a deeper unity of purpose."[28]

---

[27] Long assumed, that contention was copiously illustrated in Avraham Shapira, *The Seventh Day: Soldiers Talk About The Six Days' War* (trans. H. Near; Harmondsworth: Penguin, 1971). This volume contains several moving examples of the extent to which IDF troops (secular and religious alike) sought to retain their humanity even in the midst of battle, and stresses their particular sensitivity to the biblical injunctions against murder, looting and rape. See also Colonel (res.), Meir Pail, "The Dynamics of Power: Morality in Armed Conflict After the Six Day War" in: *Modern Jewish Ethics: Theory and Practice* (ed. M. Fox; Columbus: Ohio State University Press, 1975), esp. p. 215.

[28] Samuel Rolbant, *The Israeli Soldier: Profile of an Army* (New York: Thomas Yoseloff, 1970), p. 154.

A more up-dated review of the intersection of Judaism and military service in the IDF largely invalidates any such happy conclusion. Instead, it emphasizes the need for a far more cautionary audit of the centrifugal military purposes which religion (loosely defined) might serve and the centripetal pressures which, in fact, the same sources presently induce. A small, but nevertheless telling, example is provided by the official covering letters which introduce the Bible presented to each new recruit on induction. Originally designed as exhortations to integration, they now lay minefields of possible contention. The first versions, signed by Major-General Shlomo Goren (IDF Chief Rabbi, 1948–1971), vigorously sought to capture the high moral ground, describing the Book of Books as:

"a sturdy fortress, a fount of valour and salvation, a source of sublime inspiration and a pillar of fire to show you the way."

Goren's successor, Mordechai Peron (1971–1977), introduced only minor variations on this inoffensively rarified theme, characterizing the Scriptures as:

"the crucible of our nation, the determinant of its spiritual thought and moral behaviour, and the decisive influence on every aspect of its history throughout the ages."

But the message issued over the signature of the third IDF Chief Rabbi, Gad Navon (1977–the present), unabashedly introduces an entirely different note, at once sterner and more concrete. After only a passing reference to the Bible as "the heritage of the nation and source of its being", Navon's rendition invokes Divine assistance in battle (citing Deuteronomy 20:4) and, still more explicitly, introduces the entire text as:

"our deed of tenure and charter of ownership to our land and to the estate of our fathers."

Such sentiments must certainly evoke a responsive cord amongst many troops. However, at a time of intense and prolonged public debate over the rights and wrongs of the peace process and of military withdrawal from the West Bank, they are equally like to strike others as little more than expressions of partisan political opinion.

Admittedly, the overall picture must not be distorted. By and large, traditional Jewish motifs and symbols continue to perform a useful military service as societal solvents. Most important of all, and as was pointed out in a letter written by a secular reservist, in the immediate aftermath of Prime Minister Rabin's assassination. Subsequently reproduced as a prominent advertisement in one of Israel's quality newspapers, the IDF remains the only nation-wide framework within which citizens from religious and non-religious backgrounds still closely associate for a common purpose.[29] Nevertheless, the passion with which that particular argument was articulated — *a fortiori* that it needed to be spelled out at all — itself speaks volumes for the extent of change which has begun to take place. There now exists an uneasy feeling that modes of expression, which for decades were almost intuitively regarded as homogenizing catalysts, might no longer serve that purpose. On the contrary, they seem to be generating fissiparous tensions throughout the Force.

No single circumstance can be deemed entirely responsible for that shift in perceptions. At the very broadest level of analysis, it owes much to the matrix of pressures (noted above, pp. xiv–xvii) which have altogether resulted in a depreciation of the domestic status of Israel's armed forces, thereby undermining their image as the most cohesive of all national institutions. More specifically, the new tone also responds to parallel changes in the IDF's own corporate behaviour, whose previous dedication to its role as the country's "melting pot" has likewise

---

[29] Entitled, "A Letter Which Must Be Read", and signed by a third-year student at the Law faculty in Tel-Aviv University, the advertisement appeared on the front page of *Ha-Aretz* on 12 January 1996. At considerable length, and with great fervour, the letter took issue with the view (publicly expressed by a professor of law) that religious Israelis fell into one of two categories: anarchists or anachronisms. The "comrades in arms" known to the writer, he insisted, fitted neither depiction. What was engraved on his memory, rather, was their devotion, self-sacrifice and contribution to the common national cause.

perceptibly waned and instead been replaced by an emphasis on the attainment of more narrowly-interpreted military "professionalism".[30] But although undoubtedly relevant to the matter in hand, neither of those developments provides an entirely adequate explanation. In the final analysis, both have to be supplemented by a third. Religion is not ceasing to be an agent of military integration solely because the IDF is declining in public esteem or divesting itself of several non-military functions. Rather, alterations in the relationship between religious and secular communities elsewhere in Israeli public life have impinged upon their association in military service. In this respect, and perhaps in others too, the IDF has begun to pay the price of its unique force structure. As the late Dan Horowitz pointed out, "a people's army", composed for the most part of conscripts and part-time reservists, can only be as cohesive as is the society from which it draws its complement. Forces of that type experience little difficulty in sustaining solidarity in the ranks when there exists a broad domestic consensus, which enables them to draw upon a deep reservoir of fraternity. However, their militia structure does make them particularly susceptible to domestic fragmentation. No army can long remain immune to the polarization of civilian society. A "people's army" is likely to suffer the effects almost immediately.[31]

That is precisely what now seems to be occurring to the IDF. All the sociological surveys conducted during the past decade confirm that the cleavage between Israel's religious and secular Jewish communities, and between various sub-strata within those two somewhat amorphous blocs, are becoming steadily more pronounced. Why that might be so remains a subject of considerable debate, much of which lies beyond the mandate of the present discussion. Far more relevant are the signs indicating

---

[30] Stuart A. Cohen, "Israel and her Army: Towards a Posture of Military Role Contraction ?", *Journal of Political and Military Sociology*, 22 (1995), pp. 1–13.

[31] Dan Horowitz, "Strategic Limitations of 'A Nation in Arms'", *Armed Forces & Society*, 13 (1987), pp. 277–294.

that the religious-secular divide seems invariably to widen in direct proportion to the youth of the respondent. The contrast with the situation prevailing in other spheres of potential dissonance is stark, and instructive. Time, it now seems clear, is doing much to heal the schism between Jews of "Ashkenazi" (mainly European and Anglo-Saxon) extraction and those of "Sephardi" (mainly Oriental) origin, and thus to reduce the dominance of what was once feared to be a major threat to domestic unity. Although many economic and educational chasms still remain to be bridged, the incidence of intermarriages between members of the two groups, for instance, is now so common that it barely justifies statistical reporting. Relationships between religious and secular communities, on the other hand, indicate no such trend. On the contrary, the ticking clock seems to be exerting a negative effect.

Partial support for that assessment is provided by the findings of one study published in December 1993, which showed that the gap between Israeli Jews who do and do not profess to observe "traditional religious rites" widens by an average of some 8% when 40 year olds are compared to those just two decades younger. Mutual tolerance and understanding decreases by similar proportions.[32] Still more relevant to the present discussion, partly because of the larger size of the sample and especially because of the age group specifically targeted, are the results of a survey commissioned by the Ministry of Education in 1994. Entitled "General Perceptions and Attitudes of [Israeli] High-School Students Regarding the Peace Process, Security and Social Issues",[33] and supported by a daunting apparatus

---

[32] Shulamit Levi, Hanah Levinson and Elihu Katz, *Beliefs, the Observance of Commandments and Social Relations Amongst Jews in Israel* (Jerusalem: The Guttman Institute for Applied Behavioural Research, December 1993).

[33] Published in Hebrew in 1995 by Ya'akov Ezrachi and Reuven Gal, under the auspices of The Carmel Institute for Social Studies; Zikhron Ya'akov. This study constitutes a follow-up to: Ofra Mayseless, Reuven Gal, & Effi Fishof, *General Perceptions and Attitudes of High-School Students Regarding Security and National Issues*, 2 vols (Hebrew: The Israeli Institute for Military Studies; Zikhron Ya'akov, 1989).

of tables and charts, the Report provides a uniquely informative insight into the disparities manifest among different classes of Jewish Israeli teenagers on the very eve of their joint conscription into military service. Unburdening themselves from the statistical accessories of their study, the authors make a pivotal observation:

"The most striking point is that if there is one major variable responsible for the differences [between diverse sectors of respondents], it is not the ethnic factor (Sephardim vis-a-vis Ashkenazim), nor the residential factor (city-dwellers versus members of a kibbutz, for instance). *The principal distinction* to emerge from the findings of the present survey is between *religious and secular youth* [emphasis in original]. In almost every area covered by the survey, substantial differences were discovered between these two groupings: Compared to secular pupils, religious pupils expressed greater skepticism with regards to the peace process and its results and evinced a greater degree of animosity towards, and reservations about, the Arab population. Secular pupils attributed more importance to hedonistic and material values, whilst religious pupils apportioned greater weight to values associated with communal assistance and contribution. Religious pupils articulated a stronger sense of Israeli and [especially] of Jewish identity, as well as more confidence in their continued residence in the country....

Most of these differences between religious and secular [pupils] have become sharper since our last survey, conducted in 1988."

At times, the sheer volume of data threatens to de-personalize the respondents. Unless lubricated by cameo portraits, the dry statistics tend to exert a deadening impact and even obscure the tensions which arise when individuals raised in very different environments are thrown into close proximity by the experience of enlistment. Fortunately, such evidence too is readily available. One example, especially notable because of the audience to which it was addressed, is provided by a cautionary article which two fresh conscripts published in the bulletin of the national religious youth movement, B'nei Akiva. "The IDF", they warned younger members to be aware, "is not at all a religious institution". Only in part is this because conditions in the unit mess do not always meet orthodox dietary standards, especially in isolated front-line postings which are too small to billet a military chaplain. Far more significant are the challenges posed by other tests, most of which are all the more traumatic for being so unexpected.

"Quite apart from experiencing the shock to which every conscript is submitted on entering the military framework, the religious soldier in addition is estranged and struck dumb by the comportment of his secular comrades. Even their everyday speech contains phrases and terms which his own mouth, used to prayer, is unable to utter and which his ears, attuned to words of wisdom, refuse to absorb."[34]

VII

Subsequent chapters in this book will examine the implications of such disparities, and analyze the stresses to which they contribute within a specifically military setting. The remainder of the present chapter seeks briefly to outline in a more synoptic form three of the predominant behavioural tendencies adopted by religious troops and potential conscripts and to illustrate their principal manifestations. For the purposes of analysis, those tendencies are here labelled: (i) insulation; (ii) dissidence; and (iii) withdrawal.

1.   In the present context, ***insulation*** describes the process whereby conscripts from orthodox religious homes seek to minimize the threat which military service might pose to their continued ability to perform the various rites and practices which Judaism commands and which they wish to continue to observe to the full. Thus, it constitutes an attempt to ensure that the IDF's integrative push will not entirely overpower the disjunctive pull exerted by their own particular backgrounds.

As already noted, the *rabbanut tzeva'it* was expressly established in order to resolve that dilemma, not least by ensuring that the ambience of the IDF as a whole conforms to the minimum requirements of orthodox Jewish ritual practice. However, a sharpening of the cultural discrepancies increasingly jeopardizes the chances of success. Religious servicemen and women express growing dissatisfaction with the services provided by a chaplaincy which, at best, can only establish a lowest common denominator of observance. For their part, secular conscripts

---

[34] Ya'akov Levi and Aaron Furstein, "It is not Easy to be a Religious Soldier", *Zera'im* (B'nei Akiva bulletin), 8 (July 1995), pp. 8–9. On B'nei Akiva see below, p. 82.

tend to show less tolerance towards the dispensations granted under the *rabbanut's* aegis to religious troops who request, for instance, free time in order to pray. Altogether, in fact, the *rabbanut tzeva'it* seems to be gradually losing much of whatever influence it once possessed, amongst both religious and secular communities alike. Media gossip attributes responsibility for that situation to the age and somewhat dull character of Major-General Navon, who assumed office as IDF Chief Rabbi as long ago as 1977 when already aged 56, and who projects very little of the charisma and authority with which Major-General Goren, especially, was so profusely endowed.[35] A less mischievous appraisal, however, suggests that the causes lie in a deeper change in climate. It is perhaps no coincidence that "The Time of Trimming" by Haim Be'er, a novel which satirized the *rabbanut tzeva'it*, albeit against a background of events which took place in the 1950s, topped Israel's best-seller lists for several months in the late 1980s and ran to seven printings.

In the absence of a strong IDF rabbinate, the religious community has sought to quarantine its conscripts from what it considers to be the contaminating influences of military life by a variety of explicitly sectarian measures. As is perhaps only to be expected from a society which places so much store by the written word, many are literary in form. Privately-produced "handbooks" of religious military conduct, designed to cover every aspect of army life in both its inter-personal and ritual dimensions, are now issued as a matter of course to all national-religious conscripts as soon as they leave high school.[36] Still more conspicuous, however, has been a renewed demand

---

[35] See, e.g., Lili Galilee, "17 Years in a Peaked Cap", *Ha-Aretz*, 15 May 1994 and Alex Fishman, "The Interminable Rabbi", *Ma'ariv*, 24 May 1994.

[36] E.g., *Laws Concerning Army and War: A Guide to Students on the Eve of Conscription* (Hebrew: ed. Shlomo Min-Hahar et al; Jerusalem: Haskel, 1971). Still more popular is Zachariah Ben-Mosheh, *Laws Concerning the Army* (Hebrew: 2nd. edtn. Sha'alvim, 1988), which has been reprinted in a pocket-sized paperback edition several times. Significantly, the latter volume contains no mention whatsoever of the *rabbanut tzeva'it*, to whose functions the earlier work devoted several pages.

for the establishment of segregated military units, composed predominantly, if not entirely, of conscripts from an orthodox Jewish background.

In the case of males, this expression of insulation takes two institutional forms. One consists of the *hesder* (literally "arrangement") companies, staffed by personnel who combine their military service with study in an academy of traditional Jewish learning. The other is the network of "pre-conscription religious colleges" (*mekhinot kedam tzeva'iot*), whose students defer their military service for a year, in which they seek to strengthen their religious affiliations. Thereafter, graduates generally enlist, often *en bloc*, in elite fighting formations. (Both these frameworks will be discussed in further detail in chapters three and four, below). Females have access to a similarly sectarian institutional buffer. In their case, it is provided by the IDF Education Corps, in which a large proportion of religious female girl conscripts are placed as supplementary teachers, and which likewise enlists them as a group.

2. **Dissidence** encompasses a very much more ominous range of behaviour. Basically, this is because it makes the performance of military functions, even within a sectarian service framework, provisional on their congruence with the dictates of rabbinic instruction. In its mildest form, dissidence, as thus defined, might amount to little more than the insistence by individual servicemen and women that their officers and fellow-soldiers show due respect for their sensibilities. In a more extreme and threatening variant, however, dissidence might also take the form of a refusal by groups of religious troops to carry out certain functions which they believe to constitute transgressions of faith. As such, it is barely, if at all, distinguishable from mutiny. Mobilizing theological proofs in order to justify collective non-compliance with orders, it subordinates the authority of military commands to the dictates of rabbinic instruction.

Both of these expressions of dissidence have become increasingly prominent. To some extent, the reasons may lie in sociological developments to which reference has already been made. If, indeed, religious troops sense a growing discrepancy between their own code of everyday *mores* and that of their secular comrades in arms, it is only to be expected that they might themselves demand a more rigorous attention to details of observance which their predecessors were perhaps prepared to compromise. Certainly, many contemporary frictions seem to revolve around punctilious interpretations of comparatively obscure ritual observances, and to be generated more by insensitivity on the part of the parties involved than by deliberate intent. Hence, although occasionally sensationalized by press coverage and even topics of heated parliamentary exchanges,[37] they soon dissipate.

Other instances of mild dissidence, however, seem to have struck deeper roots. I was particularly impressed, for instance, by the disparity between the behaviour of religious and secular troops at a swearing-in ceremony which the IDF armoured corps held in the presence of an invited audience of families and other guests in the summer of 1991. The commanding officer read out the standard oath of IDF allegiance and called upon the serried ranks of conscripts to signify their acceptance of its terms. Secular troops did so in the time-honoured fashion and shouted out, in unison, "I swear". But religious troops, who comprised about a third of this particular cohort, equally loudly responded "I declare" (a rejoinder ultimately mandated by the traditional caution against a possible infringement of third of the Ten Commandments: "Thou shalt not take the name of the Lord thy God in vain"). Admirably unfazed by the resultant cacophony, or so it seemed, the commanding officer smartly saluted and continued with the proceedings. But bystanders could be pardoned some mild bemusement. My own immediate association was with crowd behaviour at an important

---

[37] See, e.g., the rumpus generated by reports that an officer had disciplined religious troops for preferring to march back to base on the sabbath, rather than ride. The deputy Minister of Defence apologized. *Kneset Protocol,* 29 March 1995.

football match. The supporters who pack the terraces are obviously there for the same purpose, and have a common interest in seeing the game played according to agreed rules. Nevertheless, their chants leave no doubt that, as groups, they possess rival allegiances.

Collective religious dissidence is likely to become a still more serious matter when harnessed for political purposes. It can then smack of insubordination. For most of its history, the IDF could afford to regard any such prospect as only a hypothetical possibility. Progress in the peace process between Israel and her neighbours, however, has done much to transform it into a realistic threat. As we have already noted, Prime Minister Begin's decision to trade the Sinai for peace triggered a religious debate over military issues as early as 1979. With the agreement of later governments to relax IDF control over various other portions of the territories conquered in 1967, polemic has become still more intense. The reasons are theological as well as strategic. By definition, all national religious Zionists regard Jewry's possession of the Land of Israel as a God-given right. Most also consider their tenure over Judea and Samaria to be irrevocable, and hence beyond the purview of government fiat. Only a very thin line might separate that belief from the contention that territorial withdrawal contravenes Divine law, and that military orders to dismantle either civilian settlements or IDF installations must therefore be disobeyed.

Precisely how much such arguments might in fact foster incidences of collective dissidence amongst religious troops will be examined in chapter 4, below. For present purposes, what needs to be stressed is that they have been articulated with increasing precision since September 1993, when Israel announced the conclusion of her initial accord with the PLO. Indeed, almost immediately after the news broke Rabbi Shlomo Goren, the former IDF Chief Rabbi, issued an explicit call to reject both the terms of that document and its operational corollaries. During the course of a lengthy statement addressed, not incidentally, to the "Council of Rabbis of Judea and Samaria" he declared:

"It is clear that according to the *halakhah* a soldier who receives an order which contradicts the laws of the *Torah* must carry out the *halakhah* and not a secular instruction.... *A fortiori* is it forbidden to obey a military order which contradicts the commandment of settling the Land of Israel, which is equivalent to all the commandments of the *Torah*."[38]

As we shall see, this injunction has since been repeated with even greater emphasis by a still wider circle of religious mentors, including some who are principals of the religious academies attended by *hesder* troops.

3.   Finally, note must be taken of the phenomenon of **withdrawal**. As the term implies, this does not take the form of a tendency to perform military service in units defined by the nature of their composition. Neither does it resort to religious arguments in order to justify a refusal to carry out certain military commands. Rather, withdrawal posits the right of individuals eligible for enlistment to defer their conscription for reasons of religious conscience, or to refuse to perform military service altogether.

As thus defined, withdrawal is adopted by two major segments of the religious community in Israel. One consists of 18 year-old males, who are excused from the draft provided they are enrolled in academies of religious instruction (*yeshivot*) and devote themselves full time to their talmudic studies. A parallel preference for withdrawal is common, secondly, amongst 18 year-old religious females, who claim exemption from conscription into the IDF on the grounds that the military environment more generally poses a threat to their traditional religious life-styles. Many of the young women thus released from service perform no other communal duty whatsoever. However, since the establishment of "The Association for National/ Voluntary Work" under the patronage of the Ministry of Social Welfare in 1970 (and, thereafter, of several similar bodies), a growing proportion of religious high-school graduates contract to perform a year or two of non-paid civic service. After a short

---

[38] Rabbi Shlomo Goren, "Disobedience to an Order", (Hebrew) *Bulletin of the Council of Rabbis of Judea and Samaria*, 14, December 1993, p. 1.

period of training, they work in a voluntary capacity as social workers, para-medics, assistant teachers, nature preserve guides etc.

Neither of these categories of exemptions is at all new.[39] As a concession to ultra-orthodox sensibilities, Ben-Gurion allowed deferments from military service to all males for whom "the study of *Torah* is their profession" even before the IDF was officially established. Similarly, provisions for the non-enlistment of religious females were formally incorporated into the amended National Service Law enacted in 1953. What has changed over time, however, are the numbers involved. Largely in response to the growing political leverage exercised by the religious political parties, the rate of draft exemptions on religious grounds has grown remarkably. Whereas in 1948, no more than a few hundred males were excused conscription, by the early 1990s the figure was in excess of 20,000 *per annum*. Moreover, since most of that number father large families by the time the terms of their deferments elapse, they become altogether exempt from the draft. Even more striking is the growth of non-recruitment in the female sector. Whereas women who claimed exemption from the draft were once required to have their applications verified by a rabbinical board, such is no longer the case. Instead, and largely in response to the argument that appearance before such a tribunal infringes on the privacy incumbent on orthodox Jewish women, girls applying for exemption on religious grounds have since 1981 simply been required to submit a pro forma declaration. Some twenty per cent of all potential female recruits are presently estimated to avail themselves of that option. Of these, probably no more than half join civil service programmes.

---

[39] Data in the following paragraph is derived from: Dov Fruman, *Voluntary Enlistment and Religious Zionism: Practical Halakhah* (Hebrew: Jerusalem: The Central Bureau for Voluntary Work and Culture amongst Religious Youth, 1991) and Yehezkel Cohen, *Enlistment in Accordance with the Halakhah: On the Exemption of Yeshiva Students from Service in the IDF* (Hebrew: Tel-Aviv: The Religious Kibbutz Movement, 1992).

Thanks to both the "baby boom" which occurred in Israel after the end of the 1973 Yom Kippur War, and the large rate of recent immigration from the former USSR and Ethiopia, the high incidence of non-enlistment by the ultra-orthodox community does not constitute a serious drain on the IDF's overall military potential. In fact, and as senior IDF sources have themselves acknowledged, so large is the current surfeit of recruits (especially in the female segment) that those young women who perform voluntary civic service undoubtedly make more of an overall contribution to society in that guise than they would in uniform.[40] Nevertheless, the phenomenon of withdrawal retains its symbolic significance. By choosing not to participate in such large numbers in what is still generally regarded as the most significant of all national obligations, members of the ultra-orthodox religious community have reinforced the marginal status which their particular codes of dress and manners in any case make likely. More seriously still, they have provided secularists with a particularly evocative excuse for tarring all ultra-orthodox practices with the brush of parasitical behaviour. At a time when most Israeli youngsters are still required to devote two or three years of their lives to conscript service, and to obey summonses to reserve duty for some two decades thereafter, the sight of so many citizens who are under no such obligation generates resentment and disdain. Thus, instead of being a shared experience which might perform a bridging function between the religious and secular segments of the population, conscription has become an issue which intensifies their discord.

VIII

It would undoubtedly be wrong to take the case too far. Even though under increasing strain, the integrative ties which tra-

---

[40] Interview with Brig.-General (Res.) Alex Einhoren, former head of planning in IDF Manpower Division, *Yedi'ot Aharonot* (Hebrew; Tel-Aviv daily), 25 January 1996.

ditionally bonded religion and military service in Israel have not yet been broken by the cumulative effect of the segregational tendencies to which they are now subjected. The IDF remains one of the few national institutions within which traditional religious rituals are still transmitted in a form with which non-observant citizens can identify. Nevertheless, there exists no guarantee that such conditions will be able to persist. Growing tendencies towards religious insulation, dissidence and with-drawal are producing variant attitudes towards military service as a mark of Jewish citizenship, not least within the religious community itself. Our next chapter will outline those attitudes and analyze their ideological roots.

THREE

The Religious Boundaries
of Military Service in Israel

Few aspects of human behaviour are as puzzling as is the extent of mass participation in military service. After all, even in peacetime army life tends to be harsh. During wars, it can also be extremely dangerous. Nevertheless, ever since the dawn of civilization, rulers and their generals have been able to mobilize enormous hosts of fighting men and feed them into the carnage of battle.

Military sociologists and psychologists spend much of their time attempting to account for those phenomena. Briefly summarized, their researches indicate a need to distinguish between at least two distinct subjects of enquiry. They sum up the first when asking: "Why do troops fight ?", a question aimed at identifying the considerations which might explain how most front-line soldiers manage to function under even the most testing of physical and mental circumstances. No single answer has been found. But the thrust of evidence points overwhelmingly in one particular direction. Very few individuals, it seems, can be (or ever have been) inured to the discomforts and sheer terror of battle solely by religious faith, political hatreds or love of country. Once the shooting starts, combat motivation invariably becomes dependent on a range of more specific stimulants. In small part, these are provided by the habits instilled during long months of rigorous training. More commonly, they derive from what is known as "the buddy syndrome": the unique ties of association which exist amongst comrades in arms.[1] Samuel Rolbant's extensive studies of battle motivation in the IDF of

---

[1] Anthony Kellet, "The Soldier in Battle. Motivational and Behavioral Aspects of the Combat Experience", *Psychological Dimensions of War* (ed. B. Glad; London: Sage, 1990), pp. 215–235.

the late 1960s suggest that, in this respect, the behaviour of Israeli troops matches that of most other soldiers known to recorded history.

"Men said that what worried them most during combat was what others [the hevrah; i.e. "the gang"] would think of them, or what their families or friends would feel about them when they came home."[2]

Matters become considerably more complicated when the questions posed is not "Why do soldiers fight? " but "Why do individuals enlist as soldiers in the first place ?" This, the second main interest of military sociology, seems to yield no universally applicable and timeless rules. Instead, the answers ultimately depend on vagaries of period and place. In some respects, that discrepancy is not altogether surprising. Much though the technological ingredients of warfare have changed over the centuries, as far as the psychological pressures exerted on the individual soldier are concerned the brutal face of battle has remained remarkably constant. By contrast, the milieu of conscription, together with the societal status attached to military service, show enormous irregularities — even within single cultures. This perhaps explains why, over the long haul, members of different societies have always enlisted for very different reasons.[3]

Most, of course, have never possessed any real alternative. Throughout history, the vast majority of soldiers have been compulsory conscripts, press-ganged into military service against their will and by whatever means of coercion the authorities could muster. But even when military enslavement was at its peak, there never existed a shortage of volunteers, eager to enlist for a variety (or combination) of emotional, material and ideological reasons. Some flocked to recruitment centers pri-

---

[2] Rolbant, *The Israeli Soldier*, p. 161. For an up-dated confirmation: Reuven Gal, *A Portrait of the Israeli Soldier* (Westport CT: Greenwood Press, 1986), pp. 143–165.
[3] Still valuable is: Michael R. D. Foot, *Men in Uniform: Military Manpower in Modern Industrialized Society* (London: Weidenfeld & Nicolson, 1961).

marily in search of adventure, fame and companionship. Others did so because they regarded the military as a profession, promising both a steady income and social prestige. In yet a third category, often overlapping with the first two, the motives were ostensibly more altruistic and derived from a view of military service as a national duty, and even a civic privilege. Enlistment allowed troops to express their loyalty to the cause for which they declared themselves ready to die (and kill), and their membership of the community on whose behalf they undertook to do so.

As all analysts of contemporary military affairs point out, throughout the western world armed forces are presently having to adapt to sweeping changes in attitudes towards enlistment.[4] Massive cultural shifts in the meanings attached to national service, together with the decline in threat perception consequent upon the end of the Cold War, largely undermine public support for the maintenance of mass-based armies. Even in such countries as France, where military service was once considered a national icon, tolerance for conscription has steadily eroded. Only rarely does this new climate create a shortage of cadres available for duty. Its principal effect has been to generate changes in the balance of motives shaping individual decisions to volunteer. Compared to their predecessors of only a generation ago, fewer soldiers join "post-modern" armies in response to either a sense of duty or in search of personal fulfillment. Instead, men (and, increasingly, women too) now contract for service as employees, and for reasons which are legitimated in terms dictated by the marketplace. Career motives constitute the principal attractions of service in the armed forces, and especially in the technical support branches upon which those forces have come to depend. The military, in this

---

[4] Extensive surveys of this field are provided in: James Burk (ed.), *The Military in New Times: Adapting Armed Forces to a Turbulent World* (Boulder: Westview Press, 1994).

sense, has become a job, barely — if at all — distinguishable from other occupations in the public sector.[5]

I

Attitudes towards enlistment in Israel have not yet assumed an entirely "post-modern" complexion. Partly, this is because compulsory conscription remains on the statute books; more substantially it is because most Jewish citizens still agree to their collective depiction as (perforce) a "nation in arms". Hence, they continue to regard military service, at least in the abstract, as a compelling national necessity.[6] Nevertheless, Israeli society is gradually divesting itself of its singularity in this regard. In Israel, attitudes towards enlistment are undergoing changes similar to those apparent elsewhere in the western world — and often for analogous reasons. What is more, the IDF is gradually, albeit hesitantly, assuming several of the characteristics of a more "professional" force.

Three trends reflect and reinforce that process.[7] One is the deliberate emphasis now being placed on material renumeration, rather than on symbolic rewards, as an appropriate reimbursement for military service. Suggestions that tax rebates be granted to reservists summoned for especially lengthy tours of annual duty indicate that this development even affects the reserve complement. But it is most obtrusive where professionals are concerned. Successive Chiefs of Staff have waged persistent — and public — campaigns to improve military salaries and expand the range of fringe benefits (housing and car allowances, bonuses,

---

[5] For early observations of this trend in several countries (including Israel) see: Charles Moskos and Frank Wood (eds.), *The Military: More Than Just a Job?* (Washington: Pergamon-Brassey's, 1988); and James Burk, "The Decline of Mass Armed Forces and Compulsory Conscription", *Defense Analysis*, 8 (1992), pp. 45–59.

[6] Reuven Gal & Stuart Cohen, "Israel: Still Waiting in the Wings", *Post-Modern Militaries* (ed. C. S. Moskos; forthcoming).

[7] Stuart A. Cohen, "The IDF: From a 'People's Army' to a 'Professional Military'", *Armed Forces & Society*, 21 (1995), pp. 237–254.

pensions, etc.) granted to career personnel of all ranks. No other course, they have claimed, could enable the IDF to attract the sort of manpower it requires, especially in such "high-tech" fields as computer analysis and electronic surveillance where skilled manpower is in any case in short supply and competition from the civilian job market is so stiff. By and large, that campaign has enjoyed considerable success. Since 1985, the proportion of the Israeli national budget devoted to defence has been slashed from 12% of the domestic Gross National Product (itself a decline from the peak of 17% in 1974) to just 8.5% in 1994. Nevertheless, the wage increases granted to professional military personnel during the same period easily outpaced the national average. At the same time, new "fast tracks" to military promotion were instituted; and the rule which once enforced compulsory retirement after just twenty years of service relaxed. Largely as a result, the complexion of the entire Force has perceptibly altered. For a growing proportion of the overall complement, what was once a part-time national duty has now become a long-term and renumerative occupation.

A second trend, similarly conducive to changes in the climate of enlistment, is apparent at lower reaches of the IDF's structure. Slowly, but apparently inexorably, the principle of equal and across-the-board compulsory military duty is being infringed. As part of its drive to economize on wastage and construct what is termed "a slimmer and smarter" army, the IDF has begun to adopt a policy of selective conscription. In the case of females, this is apparent from the proposal to reduce draft terms to just 18 months, a recommendation formally tabled in October 1994 by a high-powered analysis of future IDF personnel policies. In the male segment, it finds expression in the introduction of stiffer educational, psychometric and physical screening tests, and in a growing readiness to grant shorter terms and/or early discharges to individuals who exhibit particular difficulties in adapting to the rigours of army life. Middle-aged new immigrants and younger recruits drawn from disadvantaged communities have been particularly affected. Once drafted as a matter of course for a full conscript span, many individuals in both categories are now conscripted for only a short course of basic training — if that. Inevitably, inequalities between citizens who do and do not serve become still more marked in the reserves. Indeed, it has been calculated that as little as 13 per cent of the entire reserve complement presently shoulders some 90% of the overall burden of duty.[8]

Together, both of the tendencies outlined above have contributed to the emergence of a third: a perceptible blurring of the image of enlistment in the IDF as a necessary rite of passage to full Israeli citizenship. This is most markedly illustrated by the behaviour of prospective draftees. The vast majority, admittedly, still report for duty with considerable enthusiasm. Polled in 1994, moreover, almost 75% of Israeli Jewish youth of draft age, females as well as males, expressed a willingness to enlist for full terms of military service even were conscription to be voluntary. By almost any other contemporary international standard, compliance of that order is very high indeed (equalled, in western countries, only by males in Finland). Nevertheless, the figures lose some of their gloss if compared with the results of parallel surveys conducted in 1980, 1984 and 1988, when the results were 90%, 88% and 94%, respectively.[9] Whether the recent dip attests to the climate of expectations induced by the current peace process, or to the more insidious effects of a cultural atmosphere sometimes labelled "post-Zionism", cannot presently be ascertained. About the general trajectory of opinion there can, however, be no doubt. Many prospective draftees are still undoubtedly attracted to the IDF either by the promise of a personal challenge or the prospect of economic

---

[8] Kneset Member Ra'anan Cohen, reported in *Ha-Aretz*, 31 May 1995.
[9] These figures are taken from the surveys cited above, pp. 59–60. Data on Finland is derived from: Penetti Lehtimaki, "Finnish Youth's Opinions About General Conscription and National Defence", paper presented at the Biennial Conference of the Inter-University Seminar on Armed Forces & Society, Baltimore, MD., October 1995.

reward (sometimes, perhaps, both). But for increasing numbers, neither incentive is now compelling. In 1995, Lieutenant-General Amnon Lipkin-Shahak, the current IDF Chief of Staff, publicly admitted (to the foreign press, no less) that the rate of voluntary enlistment to some of the less glamorous combat units had been steadily declining whilst the number of "drop-outs" from front-line service in both the conscript and reserve segments was climbing.[10] In 1996, the new CO of the Manpower Branch reportedly commissioned a special report on the steps required in order to reverse both trends.[11]

The general impression conveyed by a *tour d'horizon* of overall Israeli attitudes towards military service must be modified once attention is focused more specifically on the religious communities. Within this segment of Jewish society, the situation is far more diffuse — and becoming increasingly polarized. One school of thought categorizes enlistment in the IDF as a theological imperative. For the purposes of analysis, we may classify this attitude as religiously "affirmative". It adds a powerful spiritual dimension to the predominantly supportive view of military service still deeply embedded in Israel's political culture. By contrast, more conservative streams of religious thought evince an essentially "resistant" attitude towards enlistment. In their projections, military duty is at best a tribulation to be endured; at worst, it constitutes a diversion from the true calling which Jews were placed on earth to follow. The remainder of the present chapter seeks to trace the manifestations of those two opposing perspectives and to provide some illustrations of the arguments adduced by each side in support of its own angle of vision.

---

[10] Clive Haberman, "Israel Deglamorizes the Military", *New York Times*, 31 May 1995, A9.

[11] *Ha-Aretz*, 6 February 1996.

II

An *affirmative* view of military service is most commonly found in what is known as the "national-religious" segment of Zionist Israeli society, comprising some 12–15% of the country's total population. Confronted with the challenge of modernity, and more particularly of modern Jewish statehood, members of this community (which embraces Ashkenazim and Sephardim alike) do not seek to retreat into their own insular enclaves and cut themselves off from the changing world around them.[12] Neither, on the other hand, do they accept the reductive secularist argument that, in order to live fully enriched lives in their new and independent polity, Jews must compromise the historic tenets of their faith, most obviously by throwing overboard the vast cargo of Divinely-ordained practices bequeathed by their forefathers. On the contrary, central to the national-religious ethic is the belief that the State of Israel and all its institutions can only attain authentic meaning when viewed through an essentially transcendental prism. In this view, the re-constitution of Jewish independence in the Holy Land did not merely register a milestone in the mundane political chronology of the nation. Far more fundamentally, it also defined a crucial stage in the teleological progress towards the fulfillment of Jewry's messianic aspirations. Hence, the foundation of the State warranted depiction as *reishit tzemichat geulateinu*, "the beginning of the flowering of our Redemption", an event which revealed the working of God's own hand in history. It follows, therefore, that for religious Zionists participation in the task of national reconstruction is a holy calling. Likewise, service in the armed forces expressly founded in order to defend the state from attack is a religious obligation.

---

[12] Charles S. Liebman, "The Jewish Religion and Contemporary Jewish Nationalism", in: *Religious Radicalism and Politics in the Middle East* (eds. E. Sivan, M. Friedman; Albany: SUNY Press, 1990), pp. 77–95.

The intellectual origins of an "affirmative" religious attitude towards military service in Israel pre-date the foundation of the State. At several removes, they can be traced to the "neo-orthodox" Jewish responses to modernity formulated in nineteenth century Europe, one of whose offshoots developed into what is known in the Anglo-Saxon world as "modern orthodox" Judaism. Far more specifically, however, the tenets of contemporary religious Zionism are rooted in theses developed during the first half of the twentieth century by a distinguished gallery of essentially inner-looking thinkers.[13] Prominent among this school, especially in retrospect, is Rabbi Abraham Isaac Kook (1865–1935), the Lithuanian-born mystic and talmudic scholar who was in 1921 appointed the first Ashkenazi Chief Rabbi of the Jewish community (*Yishuv*) in mandatory Palestine. Kook's singularity lay in that he did not address military service as an isolated duty, divorced from all other forms of communal obligations. Instead, he transformed it into an instrumental focus of his own novel school of mystic-messianic thought, which altogether invested modern Jewish nationalism with millennial proportions. Fired with the absolute conviction that contemporary Jewry was living out the "end of days" foretold in biblical prophecy, and that (in his own words) "the Judaism of the Land of Israel is the very Redemption", Kook had no doubt whatsoever of the steps required in order to make God's will manifest. Specifically:

"We require a healthy body. We have greatly occupied ourselves with the soul and have forsaken the holiness of the body. We have neglected health and spiritual prowess, forgetting that our flesh is as sacred as our spirit......

Our return will only succeed if it will be marked, along with its spiritual glory, by a physical return which will create healthy flesh and blood, strong and well-formed bodies, and a fiery spirit encased in powerful muscles."[14]

---

[13] For an excellent introduction to the content and context of religious Zionism: Gideon Shimoni, *The Zionist Ideology* (Hanover: Brandeis University Press, 1995), pp. 127–164.

[14] Abraham Isaac Kook, *Lights of Rebirth* (written circa 1925), parag. 33 (Hebrew: reprinted Jerusalem: Mosad Harav Kook, 1993), p. 80. In general: Zvi Yaron, *The*

For all their potentially explosive implications, Kook's teachings exercised only a marginal influence on overall religious attitudes to military service during the first two decades of modern Israel's history. In fact, it took the halcyon atmosphere generated by the Six Days' War of 1967 to provide the conditions under which their full impact might be felt. This opportunity was seized by Kook's son and most authoritative interpreter (and eventual head of the academy founded by his father), Rabbi Zvi Yehudah Kook (1891–1982). Even before battle seemed imminent in 1967, the younger Kook portrayed the IDF as:

"the army of Israel that will liberate the Land of Israel.... The conquest of the land is a *mitzvah* [religious obligation]. Hence, everything connected with it, all the various items of ordnance, whether produced by us or by gentiles... all is sacred."[15]

With victory, such themes became still more pronounced. The speed and extent of Israel's miraculous triumph over the combined forces of Egypt, Jordan and Syria, the younger Kook immediately informed his students, could only be understood when placed in the context supplied by his father's apocalyptic framework. Indeed, the troops responsible for liberating Jerusalem, Hebron, Nablus and Jericho — cities which embrace the very cradle of the nation's ancient homeland and house its most sacred shrines — had marched to a rhythm dictated by the footsteps of the Messiah, whose arrival was now surely imminent. Hence, to describe the Six Days' War as a spectacular feat of terrestrial martial arms is to miss its true meaning. The achievement was celestial and brought about by the hand of God.[16] In the words written soon after the war by one of the younger Kook's most articulate disciples:

Philosophy of Rabbi Kook (trans. A. Tomascoff; Jerusalem: World Zionist Organization, 1991).

[15] Speech on May 14, 1967, "Psalm XIX to the State of Israel", reprinted in: Alon Ben-Ami, *Everything: The Peace Frontiers of Israel* (Hebrew; Tel-Aviv: Madaf, 1967), p. 69.

[16] Kook amplified on these teachings in his *To the Paths of Israel* (Hebrew; Jerusalem: Zur-Ot., rev. ed. 1969).

"With the taking of the Temple Mount, we were suddenly thrust forward by a gigantic hand that propelled us out of the everyday and petty reality in which we had been submerged. At the same time, it seemed to us that we could not possibly absorb all the divine and spiritual force that cascaded onto us from heaven."[17]

The Six Days' War unleashed a flood of national-religious enthusiasm, which swelled into a torrent in the aftermath of the Yom Kippur War of 1973. The energy thus released found several outlets. Of these, the most zealously publicized was a programme of massive Jewish settlement in Judea and Samaria, expressly designed to ensure their retention under Jewish sovereignty and, thereby, to accelerate the progress of "the wheels of the Chariot of Redemption".[18] As Professor Aviezer Ravitzky has recently demonstrated, however, ultimately still more profound was the impact which the two wars exerted on the status of the elder rabbi Kook's philosophy within mainstream religious Zionist thought. What until 1967 had been an esoteric set of teachings, composed in the elliptical idiom of a scholastic class and intelligible only to the initiated few, thereafter became an outward-looking and missionary ideology, exuberantly proclaimed to be of immediate relevance to the entire nation.[19] That shift had particularly profound implications for the religious Zionist attitude towards military service. Increasingly (and especially in the wake of the trauma generated by the 1973 Yom Kippur war), the IDF was portrayed as "the army of God", His instrument in the struggle of good against evil.[20]

---

[17] Yoel Bin-Nun, cited in Gideon Aran, "The Six-Day War in the Religious Culture of Gush Emunim", *Israeli Judaism: The Sociology of Religion in Israel*, p. 199.

[18] Ehud Sprinzak, *The Ascendance of Israel's Radical Right* (Oxford: OUP, 1992).

[19] Aviezer Ravitzky, *Messianism, Zionism and Jewish Religious Radicalism* (Hebrew: Am Oved Publishers, Tel-Aviv, 1993), pp. 117–8. Statistics mirror the change. Even in the mid-1960s, the number of students enrolled at the Kook academy in Jerusalem amounted to only a few dozen, some of whom formed themselves into a semi-clandestine fraternity known as *Gahelet* ("Embers"); a term which itself reflects their sense of isolation. Within a decade, the register was overflowing and several "daughter" academies were established.

[20] For a particularly forceful exposition: Rabbi Yehudah Amital, *Upward From the Depths* (Hebrew; Jerusalem: Agudat Yeshivat Har Etzion, 1974). The example is

Enlistment in its ranks, therefore, constituted far more than one among the many religious obligations incumbent on all Jews. Rather, it became a paramount command, whose fulfillment — because invested with eschatological proportions of cosmic relevance — outweighed any other public duty.

III

In their most extreme form, "affirmative" religious attitudes towards military service in Israel find contemporary expression amongst rabbinic leaders of the Jewish settler communities in Judea and Samaria. Many of this group were at one time registered students in the Kook academy in Jerusalem and subsequently played a major role in founding *Gush Emunim* ("The Bloc of the Faithful"), the lobby principally responsible for popularizing the notion of "The Greater Land of Israel".[21] But the influence of their teachings is not restricted solely to prospective draftees whose parents have chosen to make their homes in settlements established beyond Israel's pre-1967 borders. In barely diluted form, they also percolate down to the mass of national-religious Israeli Jewish youth at large.

That process has been facilitated by three country-wide educational frameworks, all suffused with the posthumous spirit of the younger Rabbi Kook and all now predominantly staffed by his former students. In numerical terms, the largest is B'nei Akiva, virtually the last vestige of Israel's once-extensive mosaic of ideological youth movements. Originally founded in 1921, B'nei Akiva has long supplied adolescents with a popular blend

---

especially interesting in view of the author's subsequent record. Amital became the most prominent of Israel's national religious "doves", and in the immediate aftermath of Prime Minister Rabin's assassination in November 1995 was appointed a Minister in Shimon Peres' government.

[21] Gideon Aran, "Jewish Zionist Fundamentalism: The Bloc of the Faithful in Israel (Gush Emunim)," in: *Fundamentalisms Observed* (eds. M. E. Martin & R. Scott Appleby; Chicago: The University of Chicago Press, 1991), pp. 265–344. Also: Isaac Shilat, "The Merkaz Revolution" (Hebrew) *Nekudah*, 181 (Oct. 1994), pp. 20–24.

of scouting activities and doctrinal indoctrination; it now boasts a membership of over 50,000 boys and girls aged 8–16 distributed amongst 150 branches. The grass-roots foundation for a national religious ethos thus created is supplemented, secondly, by an extended network of predominantly residential and gender-segregated national-religious high schools (*yeshivot tichoni'ot* for boys, *ulpanot* for girls), many of which are affiliated to B'nei Akiva and all of which proclaim their commitment to the pursuit of academic excellence, secular as well as Jewish.[22] Finally, there exists a system of pre-conscription religious colleges (*mechinot kedam tzevai'ot*; see above p. 63), whose prototype was established adjacent to the West Bank settlement of Eli in 1984 with the express purpose of providing young men with whatever spiritual and physical "fortification" their forthcoming enlistment in the IDF might require. Even individually, each of these frameworks constitutes an influential agency of social cohesion and political mobilization. Combined — and many young members of the national-religious community pass through each of them in successive stages — they also act as power-houses for the transmission of a particularly intensive brand Zionist activism. The refrain to the anthem of the college at Eli (sung, somewhat incongruously, to the tune of "Speedy Gonzales") makes no bones about the message instilled:

"Yea, here is this land which I gave to you alone
Yea, here is this land which shall assuredly be yours."

Thanks to the extended series of surveys conducted between 1980 and 1994 by the Israel Institute for Military Research, it is now possible to trace with some precision the influence which this multi-layered background exerts on the attitudes of national-religious youngsters towards military service. Throughout

---

[22] The growth of this framework is documented in: Mordechai Bar-Lev, *When The Trumpet Sounds* (Hebrew: Tel-Aviv: Mizrachi, 1989). Note must also be taken of the small high-school religious military academy, Or Etzion, which also has ties of affiliations with B'nei Akiva.

that period, pupils drawn from the religious Zionist community exhibited an increasingly greater measure of eagerness to enlist in the IDF than did those educated in secular schools. Moreover, when asked to identify the frameworks chiefly responsible for inculcating a "positive" attitude towards military service, over 70% of religious respondents specified their educational institutions; a figure almost double that in the secular segment. As always, the IDF Manpower Branch is reluctant to release hard data which might confirm, or contradict, those findings. Unofficial reports, however, leave little doubt that the number of national-religious male conscripts who volunteer for placement in elite IDF front-line units markedly exceeds their proportion in each annual conscript cohort (if the grim evidence of operational casualties in the Lebanon between 1989 and 1995 is anything to go by, probably by a factor of two). Amongst NCO's and junior officers, where the selection procedures are still more stringent and service is altogether elective, the discrepancy might be even greater. At a rough estimate,[23] some 30% of all IDF fighting servicemen in these ranks now wear a knitted skullcap (*kippah serugah*), the most obtrusive emblem of male national-religious affiliation. Moreover, as many as 60% of those passing out in the first class of NCO infantry courses between 1994 and 1995 were graduates of the national religious high-school system (and, of those, over half also attended the pre-conscription college at Eli); the relevant figure in the officers' training school — itself commanded since 1995 by a religious high-school graduate — was 100%.

For reasons which probably have much to do with the subsequent behavioural characteristics of most national-religious males (in particular: their comparatively early age of marriage and subsequent attachment to family life), it seems reasonable to assume the existence of an upper-limit to their military profile.

---

[23] Yair Sheleg, "The New National-Religious Character", *Yom Ha-Shishi* (Hebrew weekly), 19 August 1994; and Avichai Beker, "The March of the Skullcap", *Ma'ariv* (Hebrew daily), 8 March 1996.

Beneath the rank of *rav-aluf* (Lieutenant-General, reserved exclusively for the Chief of Staff), the most senior notches in the IDF hierarchy are *aluf* (Major-General, of which there are usually about 20) and *tat-aluf* (Brigadier-General, of which there are currently 35). With the exception of IDF Chief Rabbis, no national-religious Jew has ever been appointed *aluf*; and only three are currently listed as *tat aluf* (and, of those, only one holds a field command). Bearing in mind the highly politicized nature of primary IDF appointments, the deliberate regulation of a *numerus clausus* cannot altogether be discounted. But a more reasonable deduction is that very few members of this community might (as yet) be prepared to undertake the long-term investment of time and energy which advancement to the very highest echelons of the military profession demands. The overwhelming majority of national-religious Jews, is the implication, do not join the IDF in pursuit of a career. Rather, the roots of their "affirmative" attitude towards military service lie buried deep in their spiritual commitment to the people, land and *Torah* of Israel, which they attempt to fulfil from the very moment they enlist.

IV

Comparisons with secular society convey only one dimension of the singularity inherent in the "affirmative" attitude towards conscription displayed by most national religious Jews in Israel. Still more instructive are contrasts with the principal patterns of behaviour evident amongst the ultra-orthodox segments of Israeli Jewish society, generically denominated *haredim* (lit. "pious", a term deliberately taken from Isaiah 66:5: "Hear the word of the Lord, ye that tremble [*ha-haredim*] at His word."). Easily identifiable by their conservative dress, and usually huddled together in specific urban localities, members of this not altogether homogeneous community comprise some 7–8% of the total Jewish population in Israel.[24] Within the ranks of the IDF, however, both male and female *haredim* are vastly — and increasingly — under-represented. Altogether, in fact, they espouse an attitude towards enlistment which is here termed one of **resistance**.

Haredi leaders served notice of their resistance to the draft even before the IDF officially came into being. As early as the autumn of 1947, a delegation of rabbis petitioned Ben-Gurion to defer the conscription of full-time male students in their rabbinic academies. On the grounds of the incompatibility of military and religious life-styles, they also demanded that all *haredi* females be exempted from service. Ben-Gurion sanctioned both requests — albeit on a limited basis. A charitable interpretation suggests that he was convinced by the argument that the new Jewish state possessed a national duty to salvage a way of life which the Holocaust had largely destroyed. Probably more germane to his decision, however, was his anxiety to include the religious parties in his emerging parliamentary coalition.[25]

Whichever the case, the process thus set in motion has since acquired increasing momentum. *Haredi* communities have grown exponentially in size and cohesion since 1948; their combined electoral representation has risen accordingly (from five *kneset* seats in 1951 to 14 in 1996). Concurrently, the exigencies of coalition politics in Israel have steadily become more acute, especially during the past two decades. Both developments have afforded *haredim* considerably greater political leverage than they once possessed. Parties representing their interests have constituted essential components of most coalition gov-

---

[24] For an analysis which places this community and its recent history in its international context: Samuel C. Heilman and Menachem Friedman, "Religious Fundamentalism and Religious Jews: The Case of the Haredim", *Fundamentalisms Observed* (above note 21), pp. 197–264.

[25] Menachem Friedman, "This is the history of the 'status quo'. Religion and state in Israel", in: *The Move from Community to State, 1947–1949* (Hebrew; ed. V. Pilowsky; Haifa: Haifa University Press, 1989), pp. 47–80.

ernments constituted since 1977; almost as a matter of course, therefore, coalition agreements have tended formally to acknowledge the *haredi* claim to favourable discrimination in all matters affecting military service. Successive legislative enactments have further refined, and enshrined, that principle. Consequently, the scope of the arrangements reached in 1948, initially restricted to just a few hundred youths, has expanded. The overwhelming majority of 18 year old *haredi* females now obtain exemption from the draft simply by signing a declaration which registers their belief that a military regimen threatens to conflict with their orthodox life-style. Most 18 year old *haredi* males similarly obtain permission to delay their conscription, and ultimately not enlist at all, by affirming that "the study of the *Torah* [Jewish law] is their [sole] occupation." The result, as several official reports note, is that non-service on the part of *haredi* males has become the norm rather than the exception. Between 1977 and 1985 alone, the number granted deferments rose from 8,257 to 16,011 (a growth almost seven times higher than that of the overall population), of whom only 288 (4.9%) and 221 (1.4%), respectively, subsequently re-enlisted as reservists.[26] Observation suggests that over the past decade the numerical and proportional dimensions of *haredi* exemptions have, if anything, become even greater.

Facile analyses of ultra-orthodox resistance to military conscription — especially when packaged for blatantly political purposes — often dismiss the phenomenon as unworthy of serious intellectual attention. *Haredi* draft-dodgers, runs the crudest version of the argument, are simply parasites. They enjoy the protection of the state, and benefit from the various social services which it offers; yet they refuse to participate in the national effort which most clearly expresses a commitment

---

[26] Yehezkel Cohen, *Enlistment In Accordance with the Halakhah* (Hebrew; Tel-Aviv: The Religious Kibbutz Movement, 1993), pp. 30–40.

to its defence.[27] Blanket imputations of this sort, although perhaps understandable, are regrettable. Indeed, they suffer from two blatant failings. One is their tendency to under-estimate the strength of the controls of social ostracism and pecuniary penalties which discourage *haredi* youth from enlisting in the IDF, and frequently disable them from doing so. Females who express a willingness to undertake military service are likely to find themselves branded as harlots, a slur which is bound to reverberate on their families, too. Males will inevitably forfeit the not insubstantial stipends, themselves largely financed by government subsidies, which all *haredi* talmudic academies grant to their full-time students; if also ejected from their parental households (as is likely) they will thus become dependent solely on the pocket-money paid to all compulsory conscripts by the IDF.[28] The second failing of most contemporary criticisms of *haredi* resistance to the draft is their tendentiousness. Specifically, they entirely ignore the extended stream of erudition which ultra-orthodoxy's spiritual guides have long marshalled in order to justify non-conscription on theological grounds.

The pages which follow focus on the latter issue. *Haredi* religious arguments in favour of exemption from military service, they will suggest, cannot be dismissed *prima facie* as nothing more than a form of rhetoric, designed to provide a smokescreen of theological respectability for social irresponsibility. Neither should they be approached as fragmentary sentiments of tangential relevance to the central concerns of religious society. Rather, they deserve to be analyzed on their own terms, as statements which claim to reflect values deeply embedded in traditional Jewish teachings. Moreover, by the criteria accepted throughout the world of traditional Jewish scholarship, their pedigree is impeccable.

---

[27] Cohen, idem., pp. 89–92 provides a representative sample of these opinions, especially as expressed by left-of-center secular political parties.

[28] Such pressures are illustrated in a rather sensationalist style in: Amnon Levy, *The Ultra-Orthodox* (Hebrew; Jerusalem: Keter, 1989).

V

In pristine form, the *haredi* attitude of resistance to the draft draws inspiration from rulings formulated by Avraham Yeshayahu Karelitz (1878–1953; better known in the world of rabbinic letters as the "Hazon Ish", the title of his first book), a halakhic guide and spiritual mentor whose towering status has always been acknowledged by the national religious community too. Like the elder Rabbi Kook (above p. 99), the Hazon Ish was born in Lithuania whence his fame as a child prodigy soon spread. In other respects, however, the two men were very different. Kook accepted the invitation to become Chief Rabbi of mandatory Palestine and threw himself into administrative work with a zeal born of the conviction that he had no right to decline the opportunity to participate in the task of national reconstruction. He reared his son on the same resolute diet. By contrast, the Hazon Ish, who was childless and did not set up home in the Land of Israel until 1933, lead an almost monastic life, declining all offers of public office and rarely leaving his tiny study in the *haredi* suburb of B'nei B'rak. From a Zionist perspective, such occasional interventions in pre-State communal affairs as he did allow himself were entirely negative. He refused to give his blessing to the arrangements (sanctioned by the elder Rabbi Kook) which enabled farmers to circumvent the restrictions which the books of Exodus (23:10–11) and Leviticus (25:1–7) impose on agricultural work during sabbatical years. Moreover, whereas Kook advocated co-operation between secular and religious segments of the Jewish community in mandatory Palestine, the Hazon Ish insisted that *haredi* society retain its distinctiveness — not least from religious Zionists — primarily by strengthening its own educational system. As far as we know, and again in striking contrast to Rabbi Kook, he never uttered a single word which might be interpreted as sanctioning *haredi* participation in national military defence.[29]

---

[29] Karelitz still awaits a definitive biography in English. The fullest source of information

As Professor Menachem Friedman demonstrates,[30] the tone set by the Hazon Ish during his lifetime has become still more pronounced since his death. *Haredi* sectarianism has been institutionalized by a truly remarkable mushrooming of "independent" kindergartens, schools and academies (a phenomenon which reflects the high birth rate characteristic of this community), devoted almost exclusively to intensive religious instruction. It has also been verbalized by an equally extensive stream of pronouncements issued by the "Council of *Torah* Greats", a fraternity of rabbinic scholars which many [Ashkenazi] *haredim* consider to constitute — under God — the highest authority in the land on matters political as well as ritual.[31] Yet, for all the novelty of the present *haredi* condition, there remains a definite and deliberately-cultivated sense of sameness about the content of *haredi* teachings. Particularly is this so when those teachings are adumbrated by Rabbi Eliezer Shach, the aged principal of the prestigious Ponovezh academy in B'nei B'rak, and since the 1970s the most powerful single member of the "Council". Revered by his devotees as the Hazon Ish's most authentic disciple, Shach has consistently insisted that latter-day expressions of *haredi* resistance to military service, especially, need add nothing of substance to the guidelines originally laid down by his mentor. Shach's own contribution has been to refine traditional attitudes and make them more explicit — sometimes abrasively so. Indeed, under his declaratory aegis, *haredi* demands for exemptions from the draft have come to encapsulate the claim of ultra-Orthodoxy to constitute the true guardian of Israel's purity and the ultimate guarantor of national salvation.

---

presently available is the multi-volume Hebrew work edited by Shalom Cohen, *The Glory of the Generation — Life of the Hazon Ish* (B'nei B'rak, 1974).

[30] Menachem Friedman, *The Haredi (Ultra-Orthodox) Society — Sources, Trends and Processes* (Hebrew; The Jerusalem Institute for Israel Studies, 1991), esp. chapters 4,5.

[31] Sephardi *haredim* possess a parallel forum: "The Council of Torah Wise Men".

VI

On purely intellectual grounds, exponents of *haredi* resistance to enlistment possess one major advantage over the "affirmative" school posited by religious Zionists. From the standpoint of Jewish political traditions, it is the former who are in the position of sitting tenants. For one thing, the principle of exemption from military service can be traced to the very earliest sources of Jewish teachings on the conduct of war. Deuteronomy (20:5–8), for instance, makes explicit provisions for the discharge of personnel whose economic and family circumstances might impair their battlefield performance, as well as for prospective troops whose "faintheartedness" could spread panic throughout the ranks.[32] Admittedly, and as early rabbinic exegesis was quick to point out, all such exemptions are waived in the event of a *milkhemet mitzvah* ("obligatory war"; see above pp. 11–33), when enlistment is both mandatory and universal, encompassing even "a groom from his chamber and a bride from her pavilion" (*Mishnah*, tractate *Sotah* 8:7). These, however, are clearly exceptional cases. As a close reading of the relevant biblical passage shows, military service had apparently been selective even during the very first recorded instance of a *milkhemet mitzvah*, the battle which took place between the Children of Israel and the Amalekites in the wilderness of Sinai (Exodus 17:9. "And Moses said to Joshua: 'Select us people, and go out and fight Amalek'.") In the event of a *milkhemet reshut* ("optional war"), the exemptions specified in the Deuteronomic code would certainly be considered valid — and, indeed, imperative. In effect, modern *haredi* thought does little more than amplify the rules of thumb which exegesis can thus distil from traditional texts and apply them to contemporary conditions.

---

[32] Maimonides, *Kings and Their Wars*, VII:9, rules that the discharge applies only to active service in the field. Exemptees are not excused from logistic-support functions.

That methodology has been most comfortably applied in order to validate the exclusion of women from army duty, especially in uniform. Indeed, in this case it becomes a medium for the re-statement of the traditional view that the Jewish female is duty-bound to preserve the distinctiveness necessary for the fulfillment of her singular role in domestic life. Empirical statements to the effect that "it is not the way of women to wage war" (originally found in folio 2b of the tractate *Kiddushin* in the Babylonian Talmud) are scattered throughout the classic rabbinic corpus; so too are dire warnings of the moral perils likely to be generated by the juxtaposition of males and females in the close quarters of barrack conditions. Medieval commentators occasionally suggested that such difficulties might be circumvented were female military roles restricted to such logistic functions as "the provision of food and water and the repair of roads." But these were minority opinions, and hardly carry the authority of explicit commands. Whatever influence they might have is countered by the absence of any indication in the biblical sources that women were ever permitted to participate in the various battles waged by ancient Israel, and indeed seem to have been deliberately precluded from doing so. For traditionalists rigorous in their dependence on textual precedents, that argument *ex silentio* clinches the matter. In the words of one recent summary of halakhic opinion:

"1. It is inconceivable under any conditions that a woman be obligated to fight in a war.

2. If a woman volunteers, we tell her to return....

3. If she does not return, she violates the [Deuteronomic] precept...

4. It is also very difficult to accept that women should serve in logistic support roles [even] during mandatory wars. There is no hint of such a role in any of the wars recorded in the Tanach [Bible]."[33]

---

[33] Rav Shlomo Min-Hahar, "The Participation of Women in War", *Crossroads*, 4 (1991), p. 234. For a discussion which disposes of the exceptions ostensibly provided by the case of Yael (Judges chapter 4) and the unnamed woman who slayed Avimelekh (Judges chapter 9): "Women and War (An Exchange of Views)", *Ibid.*, p. 247

Combined, the weight of evidence against the female military draft thus seems overwhelming. As much has long been conceded even by most exponents of the "affirmative" religious attitude to military service. Few spokesmen for that school explicitly steer the annual cohorts of 18 year old females in their constituency to enlist in the IDF.[34] Most prefer the alternative of civic service programmes — and even then (in conformity with the laconic directive of Rabbi Zvi Yehudah Kook[35]) only on condition that the provisions required in order to immunize young ladies from the contaminating influences of secular society be rigorously enforced. *Haredi* mentors, because they feel even more threatened by any non-traditional frameworks, have always been still more forthright. Indeed, as early as 1952, their political representatives precipitated a coalition crisis when resigning from the government in protest against compulsory female conscription, even to non-military national service. As far as they were concerned, any legislation which attempted to remove young religious girls from the domestic environment in which they rightly belonged directly contradicted the hallowed teaching, based on Psalms 45:14, that "the honour of the king's daughter is within".[36] This precept clearly rules out army duty. By the same token, it also prohibits female participation in public service of any other kind. Rabbi Shach has frequently, and trenchantly, warned his followers (at home and abroad) of the dire consequences likely to result from the Israeli government's decision to draft *haredi* women into civilian programmes. True faith demands that opposition to that "terrible decree" know no bounds.[37]

---

[34] One singular exception is the National Religious Kibbutz movement. See: Yehezkel Cohen, *Female Enlistment and National Service — A Halakhic Enquiry* (Hebrew; Tel-Aviv: The Religious Kibbutz Movement, revised edtn., 1993).

[35] Responsa (dated 1977), posthumously published in *Tehumin*, 3 (1982), p. 265.

[36] Emile Marmorstein, *Heaven At Bay: The Jewish Kulturkampf in the Holy Land* (London: OUP, 1969), pp. 164–173.

[37] E.g., the letters dated 1972 and 1979 to overseas rabbis in Eliezer Menachem Shach, *Letters and Articles*, vol. 3 (Hebrew; B'nei B'rak, 1988), pp. 119–120.

IV

Formulations of the "resistant" religious attitude to the enlistment of *haredi* males are somewhat more complex. For that reason, they are also considerably more interesting. They do not center solely on the individual right of the prospective draftee to preserve his or her private life-style from the contaminating influences likely to result from military service. Rather, the demand for male exemption draws inspiration from a wider vision of the society to whose perfection *haredim* deem themselves called. To put matters another way: the "resistant" attitude rejects the charge that non-enlistment caters to the particularist wishes of the *haredi* community itself. On the contrary, exemption from duty in the IDF is depicted as the mechanism whereby *haredi* males are released for a higher form of service, which benefits Jewry at large.

At root, this attitude derives from a perception of the Zionist enterprise which is entirely at odds with that posited by the "assertive" school of contemporary Israeli religious thought. Like religious Zionists, *haredim* acknowledge that the Holy Land has been divinely endowed with spiritual qualities unmatched anywhere else on earth. They also agree that residence in *Eretz Yisrael* repairs at least some religious deficiencies, if only because it facilitates the observance of certain commandments which cannot be carried out in any other portion of the globe. Where the two schools part company, however, is in the significance which they attach to the existence of the State of Israel. Religious Zionists, as we have noted, endow the State — even when administered by avowed secularists — with properties which unreservedly arouse messianic associations. *Haredi* religious thought, by contrast, adopts a much more skeptical tone. Even *haredi* leaders not entirely inimical towards the State and the profanity of its secular government (as some are), categorize their present situation as "exile in the

Land of Israel".[38] From a religious viewpoint, they teach, the Zionist political entity is no better than any other, and may even be worse. It certainly can make no legitimate claim to exceptional eschatological status.

In part, the *haredi* attitude can be attributed to the caution instilled by an awareness of the physical and spiritual havoc wreaked on Jewry by a long line of pseudo-messianic adventurers in the past. More fundamentally, it is also explained by an aversion to the emphasis which contemporary Zionism (including religious Zionism) places on physical salvation and this-worldly activity. That is not at all how *haredi* mentors envision the process which will inaugurate the promised End of Days. Exile, they teach, had been a Divine punishment; hence, a return to the Almighty's Grace is the necessary precondition for the promised Redemption. The true Restoration to Zion will signify the resolution of the spiritual dialogue between God and the assembly of Israel. In the very nature of things, therefore, it demands an other-worldly setting; indeed, it cannot be precipitated until all Jews bow to the yoke of heaven. Even then, national renewal will have to be Divinely inspired and await definitive signs from heaven that the House of Israel has indeed worked its passage home. Precipitate communal action, unaccompanied by any such omens, rebels against God's plan. Instead of hastening the coming of the Messiah, it threatens to postpone his arrival.

Only at its most superficial does the modern *haredi* antipathy towards Zionist activism warrant consideration as an exhortation to procrastination, and hence as nothing more than an extension of the political immobilism often thought to have been characteristic of Jewish public behaviour for almost two thousand years. Far from advocating fatalistic passivity, *haredi* thought in general — and *haredi* resistance to military service in particular — seeks to impart a far more dynamic message.

---

[38] Aviezer Ravitzky, "Exile in the Holy Land: The Dilemma of Haredi Jewry", *Studies in Contemporary Jewry*, 5 (1988), pp. 89–125.

At its most profound, it expresses a deep belief in the protective and redemptive properties of scholarship. Over the long haul of history, runs the argument, the scrutiny of the Holy Texts has contributed far more than any other single activity to the survival of the Jewish people. In the future too, diligent study of the Divine Law will continue to constitute Israel's primary life-line, as much to physical security on earth as to spiritual salvation in heaven. Thus seen, the maintenance of academic frameworks and the support of academic personnel who devote their entire lives to that vocation constitute supreme national priorities. By comparison, narrowly-defined military agencies of protection can be deemed secondary, and perhaps even irrelevant. To quote (once again) Rabbi Shach:

"The *Torah* was given to Israel in the wilderness... and Abraham our father of blessed memory possessed the *Torah* in Haran [i.e. before entering the Holy Land] ... We became an everlasting people before we had the "land of Israel" or "territories"....
Other than the *Torah* we have no security; neither soldiers nor the IDF will help us."[39]

V

Analysis of the received textual canon has become the prime pre-occupation of modern *haredi* society. In contemporary Israel, especially, *haredi* life revolves almost entirely around the world of traditional scholarship: the proportion of (male) students engaged exclusively in the study of the *Torah* is without precedent in all Jewish history; so too is the number of academies and the size of the market for handbooks on ritual practice and for reprints of traditional commentaries and codes. This is certainly a radical development, whose causes and sociological consequences have only recently begun to receive the academic attention which they deserve.[40] Nevertheless, the phenomenon

---

[39] Quoted in Adam Doron (ed.), *The State of Israel and the Land of Israel* (Hebrew: Beit Berl College, 1988), p. 504.

[40] Menachem Friedman, "Life tradition and book tradition in the development of ultra-orthodox Judaism", in: *Judaism Viewed from Within and from Without:*

constitutes less of an entirely new departure than an intensification of an existing thrust. In one form or another, after all, *yeshivot* (lit. "seats [of learning]"; i.e. the academies of traditional Jewish study) have served as crucibles of socialization and indoctrination for almost two millennia. Still more emphatically, devotion to *Torah*-study has always been basic to orthodox Jewish culture. Study for its own sake (*lishmah*), both of the Bible and of the multiple layers of commentaries and supracommentaries generated by the extended and intensive scrutiny of that text as the word of God and the embodiment of eternal truth, has traditionally been endowed with intrinsic instrumental value. According to some ancient teachings, it even takes precedence over prayer as a true form of Divine worship. By pondering those sources and exploring their limitless nuances, generations of sages and their disciples have stimulated and made concrete an intimate relationship with their Maker. In that way, each is said to have re-enacted the theophany at Mount Sinai, thereby fulfilling Israel's Divinely-inspired purpose. Thus perceived, *Torah*-study ("*talmud torah*") is not simply an intellectual experience, designed to collate and increase knowledge. Essentially, it constitutes a sacrament: the means whereby the Jew expresses his piety and achieves communion with his God. That, surely, is the meaning of the teaching (first committed to writing in folio 127 of the talmudic tractate *Shabbat*) that *talmud torah* possesses "no fixed measure"; it is equal to all the other activities

"the fruits of which a man enjoys in this world while the capital remains for him in the world to come."

There are two ways in which modern *haredi* thought appeals to the pre-eminence of *Torah*-study in traditional Jewish

Anthropological Studies (ed. H. E. Goldberg; Albany: SUNY Press, 1986), pp. 235–236; Haym Soloveitchik, "Migration, Acculturation, and the New Role of Texts in the Haredi World", in: *Accounting for Fundamentalisms* (eds. M. E. Marty and R. Scott Appleby; Chicago: Chicago University Press, 1994): pp. 197–235; and Charles Selengut, "By Torah Alone: Yeshivah Fundamentalism in Jewish Life", *ibid.* pp. 236–263.

beliefs as a means of rationalizing its resistance to enlistment in the IDF. First, it argues that the standards of erudition which *Torah* scholarship requires cannot be attained, still less sustained, by anything less than full-time application to that particular vocation. Every moment spent in any other pursuit, however worthy it may be, comes under the category of *bitul zeman*; a term which literally translates as "a waste of time", but which in traditional Jewish sources also carries the far more iniquitous connotation of a dissipation of the human resources which God intended to be devoted entirely to His service. Maimonides ruled that even marriage, a rite mandated in order to fulfil the Divine commandment of procreation, could be postponed if there existed a suspicion that it might divert the student from his studies. (*Book of Women*, "Marriage", 15:2–3). Indeed, on the same grounds, "that a person engaged in one precept is absolved from performing another, especially the study of the *Torah*", he went even further. Confronted with the choice of performing any other commandment and studying *Torah*, the student is forbidden to interrupt his studies, even temporarily, unless the alternative commandment cannot be fulfilled by anyone else. However, "if the commandment can be performed by others [and military service *ipso facto* falls under the latter category] he may not cease his studies." (*Book of Knowledge*: "Laws of study of Torah", 3:4). Quite simply, *talmud torah* takes precedence over all duties, public as well as private.

There is more to this attitude than a quasi-Platonic affirmation of the inherent supremacy of a contemplative way of life. It also expresses a belief that *Torah*-study, quite apart from being a spiritual end in itself, provides the community as a whole with the protective armour required for physical security. What is more, the scholastic vocation, if pursued with all the rigour that Jewish law requires, can be no less demanding than military service, requiring much more persistent mental application and just as much physical self-sacrifice.[41] Students

---

[41] The most commonly-cited basis for that view is Numbers 19:14: "This is the law,

of *Torah*, therefore, are not only defenders of the faith. By pursuing their vocation, they also guarantee the survival of the entire nation. Herein lies the second of the arguments which modern *haredi* thought employs in order to rationalize non-enlistment in the IDF. Scholars as well as soldiers ensure Israel's security. If anything, the contribution of the former exceeds that of the latter.

VI

In adherence to the rules of polemic procedure considered *de rigueur* in *haredi* circles, this argument too is buttressed by reference to precedents snatched from random homiletic and halakhic rulings scattered throughout early rabbinic texts. For instance, the principle that scholars and soldiers jointly partici-pate in the division of the labour required for national survival is traced to the talmudic commentary on II Samuel 8: 15–16: ("And David executed justice and righteousness unto all his people. And Yoav the son of Zeruyah was over the host.") "Rabbi Abba bar Kahana said: 'If not for David, Yoav could not have waged war; and if it were not for Yoav, David could not have engaged in *Torah*'".[42] Still more explicit are the sources adduced in support of the contention that scholars in fact perform a protective function in every way superior to that of military servicemen. One particularly resonant passage in the early rabbinic corpus known as *Lamentations Rabbah* teaches that Israel's salvation is ensured by the hum of children' voices in the schoolhouse.[43] Another, found in the Jerusalem Talmud and

---

when a man dies in the tent". The Babylonian Talmud (*Berakhot* 43b) suggests that the "tent" here referred to is that of the *Torah*, in the search of whose meanings students are therefore enjoined to commit themselves wholeheartedly ("to die").

[42] BT *Sanhedrin* 49a. The notion of a division of functions between the provision of material and spiritual communal needs is a prominent strand in rabbinic thought. See: Mosheh Beer, "Yissakhar and Zevulun", *Bar-Ilan Annual* (Hebrew), 6 (1968), pp. 167–80.

[43] Proem 2; for a recent discussion see: Jacob Neusner, *Torah: From Scroll to Symbol in Formative Judaism* (Philadelphia: Scholar's Press, 1985), pp. 120–2.

long cited with even greater frequency in modern *haredi* literature, classifies scribes and teachers as the true "protectors of the city" (*neturei karta*), whose right to that designation easily surpasses that of any other communal dignitary.[44]

It does not take much talmudic casuistry or rabbinic ingenuity to proceed one stage further, and to infer that the protective superiority of the scholastic function mandates the automatic dispensation of the scholar from more martial forms of communal service. Over time, an impressive range of unimpeachable rabbinic sources have been mobilized in support of that particular claim. According to one talmudic passage (BT *Baba Batra* 8b), for example, scholars, because "they do not require protection", have a legal right to exemption from sharing the cost of municipal fortifications. Analogously, *haredi* thought now contends, they should likewise be excused from the draft.[45] Indeed, on this point, Maimonides — once again the highest court of appeal — seems to be absolutely explicit. Unlike every other tribe of Israel, he writes, the Levites did not receive a prescribed territorial patrimony in the Land of Israel because

"they have been set apart from the ways of the world: they do not wage war like the rest of Israel, nor do they inherit or acquire unto themselves by physical force. They are, rather, the Lord's corps."

Moreover, he goes on, precisely the same provisions apply to

"each and every person throughout the world whose spirit has uplifted him and whose intelligence has given him the understanding to stand before God, to serve him, to

---

[44] The Jerusalem Talmud, tractate *Hagigah* 2:7. Hence, the adoption of the name *Neturei Karta* by the most extreme of the late 19th century anti-Zionist ultra-Orthodox sects resident in Jerusalem. See: Ravitzky, *Messianism, Zionism*, p. 329 n. 86.

[45] See the discussions in Rabbi Alter David Regensburg, *The Laws of the Army in Israel* (Hebrew; Jerusalem, 1949), pp. 23, 76–88. Compare, however, the virtually point-by-point refutation published in the spring of 1948 by Rabbi Shelomo Yosef Zevin (under the nom de plume "One of the Rabbis"), translated in *Tradition*, 21/4 (Fall 1985), pp. 52–56.

worship Him, to know God; and he walks aright as he has cast off from his neck the many considerations which men have sought."[46]

Placed within that framework of analysis, the exemption of *Torah* scholars from the draft does not constitute an individual and self-serving right. Instead, it assumes the full force of a communal obligation, incumbent upon all persons who have assumed the burdensome mantel of spiritual-scholastic leadership once vested in ancient Israel's priestly class. Like the Levites of old, "students of sages" (*talmidei hakhamim*) have been called to a far higher duty than military service; they must similarly be given the license required to fulfil their function. It follows, therefore, that failure to grant exemptions is not a sin for which the offending authority alone will have to pay. Rather, the penalty of Divine retribution will be borne by all Israel. Even the patriarch Abraham, a figure consistently depicted in all Jewish sources as the very paragon of human rectitude, is said to have been punished because he conscripted *Torah* students.[47] Less virtuous agencies of government (and few can be less virtuous than the secularists who presently govern the State of Israel) must certainly beware.

"If the government knew how much [*Torah*] students protect the state's well-being through their study, it would put guards in the schools, making sure that *Torah* study is never interrupted."[48]

---

[46] *Book of Agriculture*: "Laws of Sabbatical Year and Jubilees", *Code of Maimonides*, vol. 21 (trans. I. Klein, New Haven: Yale University Press, 1979), pp. 402–3.

[47] BT *Nedarim* 32a, exegesis on Genesis 14:14. "Rabbi Avahu said in the name of Rabbi Eleazar: Why was our patriarch Abraham punished and his offspring enslaved in Egypt for 210 years? Because he conscripted disciples of scholars, as it is said: 'He led forth his trained men, born in his house.'" Compare the favourable rabbinic view of Amasa (II Sam. 20:5) who is reported to have delayed mobilization in order to allow students to engage in their studies. BT *Sanhedrin* 49a.

[48] Shlomo Wolbe, "The Yeshivah In Our Era", *Yeted Ne'eman* (*haredi* daily; Hebrew), 25 August 1991. Cited in Selengut, "By Torah Alone", p. 245.

VII

Addressed almost exclusively to the introspective world of the *haredim* themselves, theological arguments which underpin a "resistant" attitude to military service in Israel articulate a point of view still shared by only a minority of the population at large. They are rejected with particular vigour by the national religious community, in which (as we have seen) a religiously "affirmative" view of military service is particularly pronounced.

That said, it must nevertheless be noted that several of the arguments which rationalize exemption from the draft on religious grounds now also permeate circles beyond the immediate confines of the *haredi* world. Undoubtedly the most interesting instances of this phenomenon (and in some ways the most ironic) are provided by the behaviour of several students who claim to be disciples of the rabbis Kook. Notwithstanding the intense commitment to Jewish nationalism which they all share, a growing number of those registered either in the central Kook talmudic academy (*Merkaz Harav Kook*) in Jerusalem or its various satellite institutions, request — and receive — draft deferments, sometimes for periods of as long as seven or eight years. In so doing, they do not of course proceed from *haredi* assumptions; the two schools of thought continue to espouse emphatically contradictory versions of Israel's past and visions of Israel's future. In practice, however, they demonstrate a parallel commitment to a shared hierarchy of theological priorities. Kookists,[49] no less than *haredim*, acknowledge the need for intellectually gifted young men to ensure that *Torah*-study takes chronological precedence over any other pursuit in life. Their request for extended deferments from the draft provides a suggestive measure of that shift.[50] In the terms employed in this chapter, it also

---

[49] A term coined by Gideon Aran, "Jewish Zionist Fundamentalism", *Fundamentalisms Observed*, pp. 265–344.

[50] Eliezer Don-Yehiya, "The Nationalist Yeshivot and Political Radicalism in Israel", in: *Accounting for Fundamentalism*, pp. 264–302.

presages the emergence of an interesting intermediary position on the "affirmative" — "resistant" axis which hitherto generally divided *haredi* and national religious attitudes towards military service in Israel.

Although still a minority phenomenon, the gravitation of some national-religious segments towards positions once exclusive to *haredim* cannot now be ignored. Especially is this so since it emerges out of a background of wider developments in national-religious society. Significantly, observers have for some time noted the need to take cognizance of a posture sometimes labelled *hardal*, a Hebrew acronym which literally translates as "mustard", but whose true meaning is conveyed by the fact that it is composed of the initial letters of "*haredi*-religious Zionists". The most visible signs of that posture are sartorial, and in particular the adoption by national religious youth of such external symbols of *haredi* affiliation as the black skull cup, rather than the knitted *kippah*. But to this must be added an altogether more pervasive thrust towards increasing rigidity and purity of observance and, above all, an acceptance of the absolute authority of Jewish law.[51] At root, such phenomena seem to reflect a growing disenchantment with the synthesis of traditionalism and modernity posited by classic religious Zionism and a preference for a reversion to the more fundamentalist roots of ritual observance and *Torah* study. Taken to their logical conclusions, they might also induce a tendency towards even greater introspection on the part of the national-religious community and its withdrawal from the wider world of public affairs. As is the case with so many other segments of Israeli society, changes in attitudes towards military service provide a sensitive barometer of that shift.

Not unexpectedly, the incremental emergence of such tendencies among national-religious youth primarily generates

---

[51] Ian S. Lustik, *For the Land and the Lord* (New York: Council on Foreign Relations, 1988), p. 166 and fn. 35 page 223.

concern within the established leadership of that particular community. Other segments of Israeli society, however, express very different fears. A growth in national-religious "resistance" to the draft, they argue, might certainly undermine the chances of reconciliation between secular and religious components of the population. Nevertheless, in the last analysis, it might prove to be the lesser of two evils. The damage likely to be caused to the fabric of the body politic by a distortion of the national-religious "affirmative" attitude towards military service is far more extensive — and certainly more immediate.

Our final chapter will concentrate on an analysis of the latter contention, and examine the specific context within which it has been raised.

FOUR

Religious Military Units in the IDF: Sources of Pride and Subjects of Concern

Literally translated, the Hebrew word *hesder* means "arrangement". In modern Israeli jargon, however, it carries the connotation of a compromise, and is applied to agreements between parties holding contradictory positions and interests. The provisions incorporated in whatever "arrangement" may be reached fully satisfy neither side. At best, they establish a framework of uneasy association which meets their minimal respective requirements.

Such is the character of the *hesder* worked out in Israel between the IDF and leaders of the national-religious community. Their "arrangement" attempts to mediate between two conflicting sets of monopolistic demands: those of the military authorities, to whom the National Security Law grants unimpeded access to the entire pool of available Israeli citizens of conscript age; and those of national-religious rabbinical authorities, who — notwithstanding their belief that service in the IDF is a sacred obligation — nevertheless assert the need for *Torah*-students to devote their undivided attention to the analysis of Jewish religious texts. The gulf between these two positions could never have been bridged had either side adopted an unreservedly confrontational stand. In fact, both have made concessions. Retracting from the position originally established by Ben-Gurion in 1948, the IDF has relaxed its opposition to the enlistment of religious conscripts in their own homogeneous units; for their part, national-religious rabbinical authorities (unlike their *haredi* counterparts) have not sought comprehensive draft exemptions for pupils registered in one of their seminaries (*yeshivot*).

The *hesder* arrangement underwent a fairly lengthy period of incubation. Unwilling to regard Ben-Gurion's original opposition to separate religious military frameworks as his final word on the subject, individual leaders of the Mizrachi party on several occasions after 1948 reverted to the theme, suggesting various institutional accommodations which might satisfy religious requisites without prejudicing state security. Not until 1965, however, were their sporadic efforts crowned with any significant success. In general terms, that timing can perhaps be explained by Ben-Gurion's final retirement from public office in 1963 and the more relaxed national security climate which prevailed in Israel between the Sinai Campaign of 1956 and the count-down to the Six Days' War in the early summer of 1967. Probably just as influential, however, were the lobbying tactics adopted by Rabbi Hayyim Goldwicht, who since the early 1960s had been principal of the B'nei Akiva *yeshivah* "Kerem Be-Yavneh" located near the port town of Ashdod. Eschewing direct representations to the highest political level, Goldwicht instead cultivated particularly cordial relationships with various senior officers in the IDF Manpower Branch. He then used those contacts as a bridge to influential civil servants in the Ministry of Defense, whom in August 1965 he persuaded to undertake what he termed an "experiment". Some thirty 18 year-old students in the "Kerem Be-Yavneh" academy, he suggested, should be allowed to enlist in the IDF *en bloc*. They would undergo 6–9 months of basic infantry training in their own segregated company and thereafter — as a group — be released for a year of study in the academy. After the latter period, they would return to their military unit for a further period of about 12 month's advanced training and duty, and then go back to the academy for two further years of study.[1]

---

[1] This reconstruction is based on hitherto classified documents in the Ministry of Defense archives. Thanks are due to Mr. Hayyim Yisraeli (assistant to the Director-General of the Ministry of Defense) for permitting access to the materials.

When proposing this arrangement, Goldwicht (who by this time had also enlisted the help of Ya'akov Drori, a well-connected official in the Ha-Poel Ha-Mizrachi [national-religious] party) seems to have had recourse to two arguments. One was in essence technical. Notwithstanding its nominal commitment to an "integrative" ethos, the IDF had in fact permitted the establishment of some homogenous military units. Most notably was this so in the case of the NAHAL [Youth Pioneer Fighting Force, see above p. 45], an infantry formation established as long ago as 1948, largely in response to pressure exerted on Ben-Gurion by a lobby representing the various Kibbutz movements, who had expressed a particular interest in using the military experience to preserve and foster the singularity of their own way of life.[2] From Goldwicht's point of view, the precedent was well-chosen. The NAHAL arrangements, he could point out, explicitly encouraged male and female troops to enlist in the IDF as well-bonded "nuclei" (*garinim*; most of which had been formed prior to conscription within the framework of various youth movements) and thereafter allowed them to serve together. Moreover, since NAHAL troops divided their conscript terms between spells of military training and agricultural work on a border settlement, they had also established a principle of non-consecutive service. Hence, there was no reason why similar conditions should not apply to students in his own academy — the first groups of which were, in fact, nominally drafted as a NAHAL *garin*.

To this argument, Goldwicht and Drori were able to add a more substantive consideration. As matters stood, male national religious youth possessed one of two choices. They could either enlist individually, and thus run the risk of succumbing to the

---

[2] The intricate process which gave rise to the establishment of the NAHAL is documented in: Yair Doar, *Ours is the Sickle and the Sword* (Hebrew; Efal: Yad Tabenkin Publications, 1992). The NAHAL corps predominantly comprised conscripts from secular backgrounds. However, the national-religious youth movement, B'nei Akiva, did promote the establishment of a number of its own *garinim*.

secularizing influences of military life; or they could take advantage of the loophole allowed by Ben-Gurion's concession to the *haredim* and avoid conscription altogether, by enrolling in one of the *haredi yeshivot*. Goldwicht's own prognosis was that increasing numbers would be tempted to chose the latter course. (His estimates were undoubtedly exaggerated — but not absurdly so. In 1965 no one could have predicted that a wave of national-religious enthusiasm would soon engulf this segment of Israeli society and thus increase the ideological attractions of military service in defence of the state). Hence, the IDF itself had much to gain from establishing a framework which might staunch a possible seepage of manpower. So, too, of course, did the national-religious community itself. Should its own reservoir of potential students indeed chose to enrol in rival *haredi* institutions of learning, the religious Zionist camp would be deprived of its most promising cadres of future spiritual leadership.

This confluence of interests ultimately won the day. Moreover, and as is often the case in public life, what began as a limited "experiment" soon blossomed into an accepted *modus operandi*. Between April 1967 and August 1968, the principals of four additional national religious academies applied for entrance into what was still officially termed "the Kerem Be-Yavneh programme" — and were granted individual permits to do so. Several others were known to be framing similar applications. Confronted with this phenomenon, and understandably unwilling to shoulder too much personal responsibility for a development fraught with political implications, officers and bureaucrats thought it prudent to raise the matter with the Minister of Defense (Moshe Dayan), who in turn referred it to a Cabinet sub-committee, convened early in October 1968. The available protocol of this meeting is tantalizingly brief and provides no record of the debate which took place. All it states is that some ministers opposed any further emendations to the IDF's existing manpower policies, principally on the grounds that a public outcry would ensue. The majority, however, expressed their conviction that the Kerem be-Yavneh "experiment" had "succeeded" — although what exactly they might have meant by that term is not made explicit. Accordingly, it was decided to formalize, unify and enshrine the "arrangement" (*hesder*) in a written agreement to which other academies were to be allowed to subscribe. The response was overwhelming. The following decade (1970–1980) witnessed the establishment of a dozen further *hesder yeshivot*, most of which were located on the West Bank and in the Gaza Strip. By 1996, the number had grown to 24, with a total annual turnover of some 3,000 national-religious student-soldiers.

No less significant than the growth in the size of the "arrangement" has been its institutionalization. As early as 1974, the Ministry of Defense decided to release the *hesder yeshivot* from their formal subordination to the NAHAL brigade. Instead, they were placed under the general auspices of the "Federation of *Yeshivot Hesder*", a non-military bureau staffed by civilian religious personnel and mandated to liaise with the academies and a specially constituted sub-unit (*mador benish*: "the yeshivah students' section") in the IDF Manpower Branch. Officially, the "Federation" was responsible for ensuring that *hesder* conscripts not on active service indeed pursued their studies. In practice, however, the "Federation" has increasingly acted vis-a-vis the IDF as both a guild and an ombudsman. It vets the applications of new academies wishing to affiliate to the arrangement, and represents the particular interests of the student-soldiers before, during and in-between their spells of military duty.

I

As an effort to resolve some of the dilemmas inherent in the possible tension between military service and religious affiliation, the framework thus developed constitutes a typically ingenious exercise in bureaucratic management. It seeks to avoid the hazards of two conflicting extremes and to steer a moderate mid-stream course.

By any accepted standards of institutional *military* measurement, however, the *besder yeshivot* are idiosyncratic bodies, which defy comparison with the conventional pattern of armed forces organization. Placed within the specific context of the IDF, the notion that a clearly defined cohort of troops might serve in a distinctive unit setting strikes an especially incongruous note. As already noted, Israel's armed forces have traditionally adopted manpower policies based on the principle of social integration, with very few military allocations reflecting the origins or affiliations of individual troops. What is more, even such exceptions as were once allowed (notably in the case of Druze and NAHAL troops, above p. 45) have over time been considerably pared down in size. Thus: in recognition of the increasing integration of the Druze community overall into the Israeli social fabric, most Druze troops have since the mid–1980s been drafted into heterogeneous units. Similarly, albeit for different reasons (many of which have roots in the dramatic depreciation in the ethos of agricultural work and a Kibbutz way of life), NAHAL units have likewise been reduced in number and deprived of most of their sociological exclusivity.[3] The enlargement of the *besder yeshivot* programme over precisely the same period, by contrast, runs directly counter to such patterns. Indeed, central to the "arrangement" from which this particular form of military service in Israel originates is the contention that national-religious troops are distinct from all others, and hence should be treated as such.

The *besder* formula gives expression to that distinction by making special provisions for three related categories of the student-soldier's military experience. One is the duration of his

---

[3] On Druze integration see: Jack Katnell, "Minorities in the IDF", *IDF Journal*, 4 (1987), pp. 40–45 and compare Gabriel Ben-Dor, "The Military and the Politics of Integration and Innovation: The Case of the Druze Minority in Israel", *Asian & African Studies*, 9 (1973), pp. 339–370. On reforms to the NAHAL system see: *Ba-Machaneh* (IDF Hebrew weekly), 4 May 1994 and report of IDF sub-committee recommendations in *Ha-Aretz*, 21 June 1995.

service; a second, the locus of his service; and the third, the conditions of his service.

1. Duration of service : Unlike all other IDF male conscripts, who are drafted for three years of consecutive duty, entrants into the *hesder* programme now contract for a five-year term.[4] Throughout that period, they are formally subject to several restrictions (such as requiring written permission from the military authorities before travelling abroad). However, they are not continuously subject to a direct military regimen. Rather, they alternate spells of study in their *yeshivot* with army service in their assigned units.

Precisely how that time-table is broken down varies from one *yeshivah* to another.[5] In most cases, the conscript spends as long as 16–17 months after his initial induction within the academy. Thereafter, he devotes some 18–19 months to consecutive military training and duty, before returning to the academy for the remaining 24–26 months of his overall term. However, some *yeshivot*, (and especially the largest), adhere to an older and somewhat more intricate pattern whereby military duty is sub-divided into two shorter terms. Under this system, the conscript spends the first 10 months in the academy; the next 8–9 months on basic training in the army; the following 12 months in the academy; returns to the army for a further 7–8 months of advanced training or line-duty; and rounds off his contract with 20–21 months in the academy.

More significant than the differences in these two systems are the features which they share in common. Both result in a situation whereby the *hesder* conscript effectively spends only about 24 months in uniform, considerably less than do conventional three-year conscripts. Both systems also mandate that

---

[4] This represents an extension of the four year programme originally instituted at "Kerem be-Yavneh". The change was announced in *Ba-Machaneh*, 7 April 1976, pp. 10–11.

[5] Stuart A. Cohen, "The *Hesder Yeshivot* in Israel: A Church-State Military Arrangement", *Journal of Church and State*, 35 (Winter 1993), pp. 116 and 123 note 25.

the initial period of the soldier's conscript terms (whether it be 10 or 18 months) is not spent in the military framework but within his chosen *yeshivah* — a feature which does much to increase the academy's hold on subsequent troop affiliations. Finally, whether or not the conscript is to perform his military duty in one consecutive term or in two shorter spells ultimately depends on the decision of the individual principals of the *yeshivot*, rather than with the military authorities.

2. **Locus of service :** The impression that the *hesder* programme provides several opportunities for the academic tail to wag the military dog would seem to be confirmed once attention is turned to the types of units in which *hesder* conscripts serve. As a rule, the IDF's Manpower Branch adheres to a strict code of placement. Once their physical and psychometric profile has been assessed, conscripts are assigned to army units in accordance with current military needs. Hence, although draftees are encouraged to state their unit preferences (and now receive a menu of possible units to which they might apply several months before their formal induction), the IDF undertakes no obligation to comply with individual wishes. This point was made explicit in a High Court judgement passed in 1991 on a case brought by a small group of articulate draftees whom the IDF had itself encouraged to attain a degree in engineering prior to their regular conscript service. The claim that this particular group had a right to demand placement in rear units where they might make most use of their qualifications (rather than in the front-line fighting formations to which they were assigned) was rejected on the grounds that the IDF retains full autonomy in this regard.[6]

---

[6] *Ha-Aretz* , 22 December 1991. The only exception now allowed applies to women who claim that they have been disbarred from certain units because of their gender. See: Moshe Weinfeld, "The Supreme Court in a Majority Decision: The Exclusion of Women from Pilot Training — Sexual Discrimination", *Ha-Aretz*, 9 November, 1995.

Judged by those standards, the *hesder* system is riddled with anomalies. Once accepted by the *yeshivah* of their choice, *hesder* conscripts are thereafter eligible for a restricted span of units. Ultimately, they can only be assigned to military sectors whose training schedules are compatible with whichever of the *hesder* timetables their *yeshivah* has elected to adopt. This circumstance accounts for the high number of *hesder* conscripts attached to the infantry and armoured brigades (where the necessary degree of battlefield proficiency can be attained in just a few months of basic training), and their relative scarcity in such "high-tech" units as those concerned with computer programming and electronic warfare, whose more specialized requirements mandate far lengthier periods of preparation. Even the minority of *hesder* conscripts judged physically unsuitable for front-line service in the field are likewise disbarred from a wide spectrum of service units, and are generally drafted into either the medical or the education corps.

3. **Conditions of service :** Like every other army in the world, the IDF makes uniquely rigorous demands of its servicemen and women. Quite apart from upholding a rule of "unlimited liability" in terms of ultimate commitment to duty under fire, it also imposes strict standards of constant discipline in matters of dress, comportment and of conformity with the orders passed down along the hierarchical chain of command. Admittedly, by most international standards, Israeli troops enjoy relatively benign conditions of service. Particularly noteworthy, in this respect, is the degree of constant contact which they are permitted (indeed encouraged) to maintain with their immediate families, by means of both frequent week-end leave passes and occasional "parents' days".[7] But even when such oddities are

---

[7] For a discussion of the context which explains this quite extraordinary degree of permitted contact between home and base, see: Moshe Lissak, "The Permeable Boundaries Between Civilians and Soldiers in Israeli Society", in: Daniella Ashkenazy (ed.), *The Military in the Service of Society and Democracy: The Challenge of the*

duly noted, it remains true that the IDF (like all other armed forces) nevertheless makes exceptionally greedy calls on the loyalty of its personnel, not least by insulating them from sources of authority potentially beyond the span of immediate military control.[8]

In this respect, too, *hesder* conscripts enjoy preferential treatment. In part, this is because of the timing of their induction into the ritual of military life. As noted above, *hesder* conscripts do not formally enlist until after they have first spent several months in the seclusion of their *yeshivot*, themselves agencies of intensive socialization. Moreover, the unique ties of loyalty to a non-military code of behaviour and practice thus forged are subsequently reinforced. *Hesder* conscripts, unlike others, are not rigidly insulated from the non-military frameworks with which they were affiliated prior to their enlistment. Instead, they maintain their ties to their *yeshivot* by the regular receipt of leaflets containing a short talmudic discourse as well as items of local academic gossip. Only marginally less frequent are sporadic visits by individual *yeshivah* principals and tutors to the students on base. Some such visits are impromptu, and the result of an individual teacher's concern for the welfare of youngsters whom he still considers to be his charges. Many, however, are initiated and co-ordinated by the umbrella council of the *yeshivot hesder* "Federation", and are thus consciously designed to remind the conscripts (and, for that matter, their officers) that this particular body of fighting personnel possesses recourse to a court of appeal quite independent of the conventional military chain of command.

Dual-Role Military (Westport: Greenwood Press, 1994), pp. 9–19. Only in the use of cellular telephones by conscripts has the IDF recently begun to draw a line.

[8] Marion J. Levy, "Armed Force Organizations", in: *The Military and Modernization* (ed. H. Bienen: Aldine: Chicago, 1971), pp. 41–78.

II

How successful has the *hesder* system of military service been? Does the programme indeed resolve tensions between religion and military service in Israel? Or might it threaten to exacerbate them? Significantly, there seems to exist no uniform response to such questions. On the contrary, opinions are fairly evenly divided between those who regard the *yeshivot hesder* as sources of pride and those who judge them to be subjects of concern. Only rarely can such assessments be directly correlated with the known religious or professional affiliations of the various respondents. Support for the *hesder* programme has been expressed by self-confessedly secular Israelis as well as by those who are avowedly religious, albeit usually for different reasons. Its detractors, too, are located in both camps. The two points of view find expression in various circles, but are particularly evident amongst three segments of the Israeli public: (i) the national-religious community; (ii) the armed forces; and (iii) the political elite. Each will here be addressed in turn.

(1) *The national-religious community*

Not at all unexpectedly, most of national-religious Jewry supports the *hesder* system of military service wholeheartedly. Indeed, spokesmen for that community frequently refer to the programme as the flagship of the entire religious Zionist enterprise, acclaiming *hesdernicks* (as the troops themselves are affectionately termed) to be "the flower of our educational system". Despite the hyperbole, much of the praise can easily be understood. For one thing, it rests on an appreciation of the function which *hesder yeshivot* serve as agencies of institutional reproduction. They supply a steady stream of teachers to national-religious high schools, themselves "feeders" to the *hesder* system, and annual cohorts of role models to whom national religious youth can most comfortably relate. Of even greater importance is *hesder*'s contribution to the national-religious ideology. Its graduates appear to embody precisely the sort of synthesis which religious Zionism has always espoused. They demonstrate, and perhaps even prove, that young orthodox males can indeed fulfil both their religious duty to *Torah*-study and their civic obligation to participate in national defence, without compromising either of those obligations. As a particularly articulate principal of the largest *yeshivat hesder* once informed a north American audience:

"Optimally, Hesder does not merely provide a religious cocoon for young men fearful of being contaminated by the potentially secularizing influences of general army life-although it incidentally serves this need as well. Hesder at its finest seeks to attract and develop *b'nei torah* [literally: "sons of *Torah*"; i.e. scholars] who, given the historical exigencies of their time and place, regard this dual commitment as both a privilege and a duty; who, in comparison with their non-Hesder confreres love not (to paraphrase Byron's Childe Harold) Torah less but Israel more. It provides a context within which students can focus upon enhancing their personal spiritual and intellectual growth while yet heeding the call to public service, and it thus enables them to maintain an integrated Jewish existence."[9]

For all the eloquence, erudition and stylistic verve of their expression, such arguments have not won universal acceptance amongst religious Zionists. If anything, the *hesder* programme has yet to prove its credentials — not least on ideological grounds. Not all lay leaders of the national-religious community feel entirely comfortable with a system which permits religious young men to spend less time in military service than do secular troops, and thereby lays their entire constituency open to charges that it is not shouldering its full share of the national security burden.[10] Several rabbinic leaders voice an entirely different concern.

[9] Rabbi Aaron Liechtenstein (principal of the "Har Etzion" Academy at Gush Etzion), "The Ideology of Hesder", *Tradition*, 19 (1981), pp. 199–217.

[10] This feeling was particularly pronounced in the religious kibbutz movement, which in 1978 persuaded the IDF to recognize an alternative system, (known as *shiluv* [lit. "integration"]), whereby religious youth divide a five year term between two years in a *yeshivah* and three full years in non-segregated military units. Only about fifty conscripts per year enlist in that scheme. More popular are the pre-conscription religious colleges (above p. 83), which precede regular enlistment with just one year of religious instruction.

What troubles them is not the possibility of social stigma but the threat of scholastic retardation. No committed Jew, they point out, can possibly ignore the axiomatic priority which traditional Jewish teachings attach to *Torah*-study as a full time avocation. Any attempt to rationalize a relaxation of that norm carries the whiff of apologia, even when it appeals to state security and proposes no more than a truncated spell of army service. Arguing from that position, even the younger rabbi Kook defined *hesder* as very much an option of the last resort. Gifted *Torah* students, he advised, should apply to the military authorities for permission to defer their conscription for several years, during which they should attend full-time "senior academies" (*yeshivot gevohot*):

"which are the principal means of increasing *Torah* and enhancing its glory. The *yeshivot hesder*, which take account of military necessity, are of secondary value in elevating the splendour of the *Torah*." [11]

Precisely the same hierarchy is now being advocated, with equal conviction and often at considerably greater length, by a number of more recent authorities. That development can hardly be justified by the discovery of any new data in the halakhic sources which debate the relative merits of scholarly and military duties. If anything, the arguments are usually repetitious and rake over ground already well-covered as early as 1948. More influential (albeit often unspoken) seems to be a heightened sense of the need to counter the growing challenge to religious Zionism implicit in the resurgence of *haredi* Jewry and in its claim to constitute the authentic repository of Jewry's scholastic tradition.

"We should not relegate Torah study to those who are not cognizant of God's deliverance [i.e. *haredim*].... In order to promote great Torah authorities [of our own], those absorbed in Torah must be freed from any other yoke.... If [they] are required to combine their study with military service, even for a very limited time, and thereafter be called to

---

[11] "Short Letters" (no date), in: *Army and Yeshivah: A Collection of the Words of Our Rabbi, Rabbi Zvi Yehudah Kook* (Hebrew; Jerusalem: Ateret Kohanim, 1993), p. 48.

reserve duty... the possibility of producing the top quality Torah leadership that our nation needs, will be seriously impaired." [12]

An increasing proportion of national-religious draftees seem to share that view, and hence (as noted above, pp. 102–104) to apply to the IDF for extensive deferments from service in order to complete a lengthy course of *yeshivah* study before their enlistment. The numbers, although still very small overall, are nevertheless steadily rising, especially among students registered in institutions affiliated with the central Kook academy. Should that trend continue, the *hesder* programme might altogether lose much of its aura and appeal.

(2) *Military Opinion*

A survey of military comments on the *hesder* programme reveals similarly divergent views. By and large, senior IDF sources express satisfaction with the "arrangement". In part, the reasons are negative. *Yeshivot hesder*, some argue, have reduced the potential loss of religious recruits, who might otherwise either enlist under duress, or feel compelled to follow *haredi* practice and claim exemption from the draft in order to pursue their studies.[13] But that contention is generally supplemented by more affirmative considerations. Thanks perhaps to the high level of religious commitment with which *hesder* conscripts approach military service, they tend to make especially good soldiers. Moreover, the units in which they serve are particularly cohesive formations, distinguished by the existence of powerful bonds of comradeship amongst like-minded troops forged during the long hours spent together in the cloistered atmosphere of the academy (and in many cases even earlier,

---

[12] Rav Zalman Melamed, "Producing Torah Leadership", *Crossroads*, 4 (1991), pp. 65–72 (compare the editor's comment on page 67); and Rav Yehudah Shaviv, "Conflicting *Mitzva* Obligations (Halakhic Aspect of the *Hesder*)", *ibid.*, 1 (1987), pp. 187–199.
[13] Personal communication: Brig-General Yitzchak Fuchs, deputy commander of IDF Manpower Branch, April 1995.

by virtue of their membership in the same youth movement and school system).

From a military standpoint, unit cohesion of that order confers several advantages. For one thing, it moderates tendencies towards inter-personal friction in the highly-pressured and stressful atmosphere which barrack conditions can often induce. Secondly, the existence of so strong a web of personal ties helps to create the "buddy syndrome" which, as we have already noted, has long been regarded as an essential prerequisite of combat effectiveness. The programme of *hesder* recruitment is said to confer both benefits. *Hesder* troops register a very low incidence of petty theft or "ragging" in boot-camp (behaviour presumably in any case discouraged, if not altogether precluded, by the religious standards which *Torah* students ipso facto profess). Instead of vying with each other for the easier assignments and for release from the more irritating chores with which army life is studded, such as guard duty and latrine maintenance, *hesder* troops invariably display exceptional willingness to rotate such tasks. What is more, they frequently manage to do so without explicit encouragement from their unit commanders, who are thus spared the inconvenience of having to adjudicate competing claims for preferential treatment. Most important of all, and no doubt as a consequence of the mutual support-system thus created, *hesder* units — as units — also perform well under fire. One striking illustration was provided by the skill and determination with which *hesder* tank units engaged a heavy concentration of Syrian armour during a particularly stiff bout of fighting in the Lebanon in June 1982.[14]

On occasion, however, praise for the performance of *hesder* troops is diluted by criticism of the difficulties to which their programme gives rise. Interviews conducted in both 1991 and 1995 with several junior officers and NCO's assigned to train

---

[14] On which see: Ze'ev Schiff and Ehud Ya'ari, *Israel's Lebanon War* (New York: Simon & Schuster, 1984), pp. 173–179.

besder units revealed an under-current of dissatisfaction with the "arrangement". Even those who themselves came from orthodox religious backgrounds (and the majority of personnel assigned to train *besder* units do not), reported that they found their tasks fraught with potential hazards. All praised the levels of proficiency attained by *besder* troops. But very few empathized with the need to make special *collective* organizational provisions for such religious needs as the commandment to take breaks in order to conduct communal prayers three times each day, or for reduced physical exertions on prescribed fast days — all of which have to be built-in to the training schedule. NCO's, especially, likewise objected to the frequency with which their charges enjoyed more summary intermissions in basic training, a privilege of which other conscripts dare hardly dream, caused by the random visits which *yeshivah* tutors make to the base. To categorize such complaints as nothing more than an insistence on the niceties of military etiquette is to miss their true meaning. In effect, they reflect a deeper commitment to maintaining the organizational chain of command upon which all military discipline ultimately depends. No parade-ground sergeant can be expected to approve of a system which might encourage a particularly articulate cohort of troops to circumvent his authority by appealing to their *yeshivah* principals and, in the last resort, to God.

Whilst lower rungs of the IDF ladder thus find the *besder* programme generally vexatious, some middle-rank sources view it as a more specific hindrance to overall military efficiency.[15] Particular concern is aroused by the limitations which the *besder* time-table imposes on both flexibility in planning and on the maximum utilization of human resources. Precisely because *besder* conscripts make such good soldiers, it is argued, the IDF ought to be allowed to make more use of their talents. At its most rudimentary level, this criticism of the *besder* programme

---

[15] Interview with Colonel Daliyah Chen, of the IDF *mador benish*; spring 1996.

translates into an assessment that the enlistment of *hesder* troops for a full three-year term of conscript service could allow substantial reductions in the burdens of reserve duty borne by other citizens.[16] More sophisticated, by far, is the claim that the *hesder* system results in dislocations which also impair military proficiency at a conscript level. As has been seen, the *hesder* soldier's alternating time-table *ab initio* restricts the span of units to which he can usefully be assigned. Even within those units, the same constraint might also impede his battle-readiness, especially if the terms of military service are sub-divided. Sedentary study, after all, can hardly be conducive to the maintenance of his physical fitness or of the technical skills which modern weaponry demands. Moreover, the interruption of a *hesdernick's* army service by lengthy spells of talmudic learning in the *yeshivah* altogether imparts on aura of transience to his military experience and thus reinforces his sense of separateness from the Force of which he is supposed to feel a part.

Several of these difficulties might be overcome were all the *yeshivot* to adopt the schedule which provides for a single extended period of military duty (which is one reason why that particular system was originally introduced). But even in that case, other drawbacks would remain. Primary among these, certainly from the IDF's viewpoint, are the inherent tensions created by the conflicting demands which the *yeshivot* and the military continue to make on the individual serviceman's talents. On enlistment, fully eighty per cent of *hesder* conscripts are considered to meet standard IDF criteria for officer recruitment (more than double the ratio in the Force overall). Nevertheless, no more than twenty-five percent fulfil that promise by volunteering to enlist in an officer's course after completing their initial periods of professional military training and a three-month NCO's programme. Most analyses attribute that discrepancy

---

[16] Brig.-Gen. (res.) Alex Einhoren (former head of planning in IDF Manpower Branch), *Yedi'ot Aharonot* (Hebrew; Tel-Aviv daily), 25 January 1996.

to the peculiarities of the *hesder* framework. All applicants to the IDF junior officers' course undertake to "sign on" for an extra year of paid professional service on completion of their conscript terms, an obligation which many secular troops, too, find daunting. But *hesdernicks* have to meet two further conditions. Before registering for the officer's course, they need to obtain written permission from their *yeshivah* principals, who can (and often do) veto the request on the grounds that the outflow of too large a proportion of their student body will adversely affect the health of their own institution. Furthermore, and even if permission is granted, the *hesdernick* also has to guarantee to extend his term of *yeshivah* study in proportion to the additional amount of time which he spends in the army. This can be an altogether discouraging prospect, since it implies that by the time he has discharged his combined obligations and prepares to embark on a civilian career the candidate will already be twenty-four, an age by which many have married, and thus some three years older than the average Israeli youngster of similar station. Such deterrents can only be moderated, it is claimed, by reforming the system of dual-control which is *hesder*'s most pronounced organizational characteristic.

(3) *The Political Elite*

Although initially somewhat reluctant to sanction the *hesder* programme, Israel's political elite soon overcame its hesitations. Indeed by the early 1980s, at the latest, secular as well as religious opinion in the kneset (Israel's parliament) was almost unanimously favourable. Reserve soon gave way to warmth, and eventually resulted in public acclaim. An apogee was attained in 1991, when a committee established by the Minister of Education (not incidentally, himself a member of the National Religious Party) awarded the *yeshivot hesder* the prestigious Israel Prize, the country's highest public recognition for unique contributions to the texture of national life. At a ceremony held on Independence Day in the presence of the President, the Prime

Minister and numerous other dignitaries, Rabbi Goldwicht received a citation which expressly noted the degree to which *hesder* troops

"fulfil the Zionist vision in their own unique fashion, by combining the scroll and the sword [*safra ve-saifa*] and being sons of *Torah* as well as men of valour. Graduates of the programme have excelled in their self-sacrifice and play a full role in the life of the country and in carrying out whatever missions the state demands. They combine the study and observance of the *Torah* of Israel with settlement of the land of Israel and love of the people of Israel."[17]

Since the mid–1990s, the tide of opinion has rapidly turned. Although the military competence displayed by individual *hesder* troops still commands considerable respect among the political elite and the public at large, the programme within which they serve has become the subject of increasingly vocal criticism, pervaded by an aroma of fear and ill-will. Censure reached a peak during the latter half of 1995 when Mr. Orri Orr, a retired Brigadier General and then the chairman of the Kneset's Foreign Affairs and Security Committee (he was subsequently appointed deputy Minister of Defense), on several occasions explicitly advocated that the *hesder* units be disbanded. His suggestion was echoed by some of the most widely-respected of Israeli military analysts. Many generally decried the admixture of "political-military" incompatibles facilitated by the programme. Others, more specifically, exhorted the government to take a leaf out of Ben-Gurion's book. Israel's first prime minister, they recalled, had in 1948 broken up the *Palmach* (the elite fighting force established during the mandate period, see above p. 44), on the grounds that no IDF unit should possess an ideological or institutional allegiance of its own. The *hesder* units, because they contravene that cardinal rule, deserve the same fate.[18]

---

[17] Ministry of Education, *Israel Prizes, 1991: Citations* (Hebrew; Jerusalem, 1991), pp. 24–5.
[18] For reports of Orr's suggestion see: *Ha-Aretz* (Tel-Aviv Hebrew daily), 5 July 1995 and 11 December 1995. For press approval: Dan Kislev, "To Disband this Palmach", *ibid.*, 11 July 1995 and Ze'ev Schiff, "A Dangerous Arrangement", *ibid.*, 11 December 1995.

Swings of that dimension in the pendulum of attitudes towards the *hesder* cannot be attributed merely to the vagaries
of mood to which Israeli politicians and their public are notoriously
prone. They also reflect an uneasy feeling that, should religious push ever come to military shove, *hesder* troops might
in the future imperil the state as much as they were once thought
to contribute to its security. Such fears undoubtedly increased
in the wake of Prime Minister Yitzchak Rabin's assassination
in November 1995 by a one-time *hesder* graduate, not least
since the assailant himself subsequently claimed to have acted
under the inspiration of an ideological commitment to the doctrine
of the "Greater Land of Israel" and with the implicit sanction
of opinions expressed by some — unspecified — rabbinic
authorities. ("Without a halakhic decision... on the part of several
rabbis with whom I am acquainted, I would have found it difficult
to commit murder. It would have been hard for me to act without
[moral] support and without a feeling that many people were
behind me.")[19] For all its impact, however, the assassination
alone cannot be held entirely responsible for the cloud of suspicion
hovering over the *hesder*. Significantly, Orr's disapprobations
of the programme did not await that particular event. They
were triggered, rather, by misgivings of a more general nature,
to which attention must now be turned.

III

All governments possess sound reasons for harbouring deep
misgivings about the armed forces which the needs of national
defence require them to establish.[20] By entrusting a monopoly
of legitimate violence to an organized body of well-trained
personnel, they in fact create a double-edged sword. Ideally,
of course, soldiers will resort to action only against targets,

---

[19] Yigal Amir's testimony before the official commission of enquiry into the assassination; reported in *Ha-Aretz*, 29 March 1996.

[20] Still an excellent introduction is: Samuel P. Huntington, *The Soldier and the State: The Theory and Practice of Civil-Military Relations* (New York: Vintage Books, 1957).

domestic or foreign, which the civilian authorities specifically declare to be enemies of the state. Nevertheless, there always exists a danger that the military, in part or in whole, might assume independent responsibility for defining the precise identity of the nation's foes. Still worse, in extreme circumstances (although in some regimes quite frequently), troops might go as far as to take concerted action against the civilian government itself, often on the grounds that their nominal constitutional masters are pursuing policies ultimately inimicable to the true national interest. At its most benign, such action could consist of the use of military influence merely as a means of political persuasion, designed to bring about a change of policy course on the part of the incumbent government. But there also exists a wider spectrum of more drastic courses: public expressions of military discontent; military intrigues designed to form alliances of convenience with disaffected civilian groupings; and, in the last resort, a concerted military attempt to supplant the existing administration and replace it with one thought to be more advantageous to the national interest, or even with an outright military regime.[21]

A variety of factors can determine the extent and range of military interventions in public affairs.[22] Much depends on the dominant political culture of the society in which the armed forces operate, and especially on the extent to which that culture (for whatever reasons) bestows on the military a mantle of inherent legitimacy not accorded to other state institutions. Much, too, depends on the corporate self-image fostered by professional soldiers, who often regard themselves as the guardians

---

[21] Samuel Finer, *The Man on Horseback: The Role of the Military in Politics* (London: Pall Mall, 1982).

[22] The major theories were summarized in: David C. Rapoport, "A Comparative Theory of Military and Political Types", in: S. P. Huntington, *Changing Patterns of Military Politics* (New York: Free Press, 1962), pp. 71–100. For a survey of more recent research: Martin Edmonds, *Armed Services and Society* (Boulder: Westview Press, 1990), pp. 93–112.

of the state and the rightful arbitrators of its fortunes. Analysis suggests, however, that the likelihood of military intervention in politics is further exacerbated by the simultaneous presence of two additional variables. One is the fragmentation of civilian society, itself often a reflection of fundamental differences within the population at large with respect to national policies and procedures. The other is the cohesiveness of a particular segment within the armed forces, whose commitment to its own code of values transcends its allegiance to the government which soldiers swear to serve.

Current criticisms of the *hesder* programme articulate an awareness of the extent to which, of late, both conditions have become increasingly relevant to Israel's situation. The broad agreement on security issues once considered a hallmark of Israeli society has been unmistakably undermined, perhaps irremediably so. At the same time, the posture of non-partisan neutrality previously nurtured by personnel in IDF uniform (conscripts, reservists and regulars alike) has steadily given way to forthright expressions of political opinion. Clearly interdependent, these twin developments largely stem from the same source. At root, both reflect the deep fissures generated in the traditional Israeli consensus on security affairs by increasing public controversy over the rights and wrongs of IDF operations, especially when conducted against Palestinians.

The stages in that process can clearly be demarcated. Signs of dissent in the ranks initially appeared during the Lebanon War of 1982–1985 when, for the first time, IDF servicemen disobeyed summonses to duty. In 1982–1983 alone, 86 reservists (by Israeli standards, an unprecedentedly high number) registered their conscientious objection to the campaign by absolutely refusing orders to report for active service in the Lebanon; it is estimated that as many as five times that number gave formal or informal notice of their intention to do so, thereby reportedly compelling the IDF to withdraw their call-up papers. One brigade commander went as far as to resign his

commission in the midst of battle.[23] The *intifadah* (1987–1993)
witnessed similar phenomena, sometimes in even more intensive form. According to official IDF statistics, 181 conscripts
and reservists were placed on trial prior to 1993 for refusing
orders to serve in "the territories"; many more (although, again,
the numbers cannot be computed with any precision) evinced
what became known as "grey conscientious objection", usually
by informing their commanding officer's of their attitudes and
requesting transfers to other duties.[24] Despite these developments, conscientious objection undoubtedly remained a marginal
phenomenon in Israeli military life, still limited to the periph-
eries of the overall complement and still entirely unrecognized
in military law (other than in the case of religious women).
But by the end of the 1980s it had clearly emerged from the
closet of political discourse and was no longer taboo. Quite
apart from being advocated by such extra-parliamentary pressure groups and watch-dogs as *Yesh Gevul* ("There is a Limit")
and *B'TSELEM* (The Israel Information Center for Human Rights
in the Occupied Territories), the right to ideologically-moti-
vated conscientious objection also appeared intermittently on
the agendas of the more liberal knesset factions.[25]

Until the late 1980s, almost all the IDF citizen-soldiers who
objected to military service on grounds of conscience professed
left-wing political opinions. During the course of the past decade,
however, the main locus of conscientious objection has shifted
to the right of the Israeli ideological spectrum. That change,
first evident during the latter stages of the *intifadah*, became

---

[23] Reuven Gal, "Commitment and Obedience in the Military: An Israeli Case Study",
Armed Forces & Society, 11 (1985), pp. 553–564; and Ruth Linn,"Conscientious Objection
in Israel during the War in Lebanon", *ibid*, 12 (1986), pp. 489–512. For earlier
periods: Martin Blatt (ed.), *Dissent and Ideology in Israel: Resistance to the Draft*
(London: Ithaca Press, 1975).

[24] Aryeh Shalev, *The Intifada: Causes and Effects* (Tel-Aviv: Jaffee Center for Strategic
Studies, 1991), pp. 123–8.

[25] *The Limits of Obedience: The 'Yesh Gevul' Movement* (Hebrew; eds. Ishai and Dina
Menuchin; Tel-Aviv: Siman Kria'a, 2nd. edtn., 1989), pp. 7–16.

especially pronounced once the Arab-Israel peace process was invigorated by the Oslo accord between the Rabin government and the PLO in September 1993. The prospect that the Palestinian Authority would eventually gain control over much (perhaps all) of Judea and Samaria aroused visceral emotions, surpassing all other issues as the single most definitive fault-line between Right and Left in the Israeli public in general. As we have seen (above pp. 65–66), feelings in the national-religious community ran particularly high, and were almost immediately translated by some quarters into a determination to use conscientious objection as a weapon in a wider campaign of public protest. As much is evident from an open letter which a junior officer in the reserves addressed to Rabin (in his capacity as Minister of Defense) almost as soon as the ink on the Oslo agreement was dry.

"As a Jew faithful to the command of the God of Israel and to the historic expression of the will of His people throughout the generations... I absolutely refuse to co-operate with any government, Gentile or Jewish, which takes steps to remove the people of Israel from its land....

The Land of Israel is an absolute value — in national and religious terms, and not merely for security reasons.... The State of Israel is [also] a value. But that does not justify total identification with all its orders and institutions.... We must break the conventions and establish new rules of struggle. No conventional activity will help. Hence, we are compelled to seek new methods... of which the most blunt is a refusal to carry out orders which are inherently illegal." [26]

IV

Critics of the *besder* "arrangement" fear that the units involved, because of both their sociological configuration and bonds of camaraderie, might be particularly susceptible to similar sentiments. Especially is this so since several of the national religious spiritual guides whose teachings *besdernicks* are thought to consider authoritative have so frequently been equally outspoken.

---

[26] Karpel's letter was published in *Nekudah*, no. 171 (September 1993), pp. 22–23. The same issue also carried three rabbinic denunciations of Karpel's action.

As has already been noted, probably the first rabbinic figure to pitch himself openly into the maelstrom of religious-military controversy was Rabbi Shlomo Goren, himself a former senior IDF chaplain. Responding to the Oslo agreement with undisguised passion (and with a verve which also expressed his characteristic relish for the slings and arrows of public debate in any form), Goren composed a copiously footnoted halakhic ruling which categorically prohibited the surrender of Jewish dominion over any portion the Land of Israel, and which therefore forbad religious troops to participate in all operations designed to implement the transfer of territorial sovereignty to Palestinian jurisdiction.[27] Where one of the recognized giants of national religious opinion chose to lead, others soon followed. Late in March 1994, a similar directive was published by a triumvirate of rabbinic authorities, one of whom was a former Ashkenazi Chief Rabbi and principal of the central Kook academy in Jerusalem, another the founding father of the B'nei Akiva network of high-school *yeshivot*, and the third one of national-religious Jewry's most respected ideologues.[28] Matters reached a new pitch in May 1995, when a group of fifteen national-religious mentors who termed themselves "The Union of Rabbis on Behalf of the People of Israel and the Land of Israel" issued a manifesto of their own.

In many respects, the latter document is the least erudite of all the rabbinic pronouncements of military relevance. It is also the shortest, consisting of just two sides of liberally spaced text. Nevertheless, it remains probably the most far-reaching and influential in its implications. One reason lies in the precision with which it addressed the problems to which the

---

[27] For Goren's ruling see above, p. 65. It was also reprinted in *Ha-Aretz*, 17 January 1994. Prior to Oslo, too, Goren had insisted on the intrinsic holiness of Judea, Samaria and the Gaza Strip. However, he had made no mention of the possibility that troops might have to disobey orders to evacuate those regions. Goren, "The Halakhic Status of Judea, Samaria and the Gaza Strip", *Ha-Tzofeh*, 20 November 1992.

[28] *Ha-Tzofeh*, 30 March 1994. For a particularly sensitive reaction see: Ya'akov Medan, "Between Refusal and a Tear" (Hebrew), *Nekudah*, 177 (April 1994), pp. 42–45.

implementation of the Oslo agreements were likely to give rise. Unlike their predecessors, the members of the "Union" did not restrict their remarks to general speculations about the possible shape of an Israeli withdrawal from "the territories." Instead, they explicitly referred to the probability that IDF troops might be ordered to dismantle military installations as well as Jewish settlements. Secondly, and again unlike their predecessors, members of the "Union" did not limit themselves to the conventional channels of publication. In addition to calling a press conference and granting extensive media interviews, they also had their manifesto reprinted on a massive scale in leaflet form and distributed to synagogues and academies throughout the country. Still more important, certainly in the present context, was the composition of the body. Amongst the fifteen members of the "Union" were three principals of *yeshivot hesder* and two other rabbis employed as teachers in institutions of that name. For all these reasons, their manifesto immediately became a milestone in the history of relations between the national religious community and the IDF. As such, it warrants analysis in further detail.

In the preamble to their document, the "Union of Rabbis" define their manifesto as a "responsum" (*teshuvah*), a term designed to strike an immediate cord of recognition amongst an audience for whom this genre of rabbinic communication carries the full weight of authority imparted by centuries of tradition. Their own statement follows the approved style. Composed "after analysis of the subject in all its aspects" and "in response to enquiries from citizens and soldiers from all sectors of the public", it is studded with references to authoritative medieval sources (including, inevitably, the traditional genuflection to Maimonides) and closes with an equally statutory quotation from the weekly portion of the Pentateuch reading. The only departure from convention is the attachment of a supplementary commentary to the formal text — an addition itself indicative of the authors' self-awareness of the public furor which their statement was likely to arouse. They had good reason to take such precautions. Notwithstanding the conciliatory tone struck in the final clause of the manifesto (which re-affirms the rabbis' commitment to educate their pupils to serve in the IDF), the main body of the text remains an uncompromising attestation of the supremacy of religious teachings to all other sources of authority. More specifically, it constitutes an unconcealed instruction to troops to disobey military orders.

"We determine that the *Torah* forbids the dismantlement of IDF bases and [their] transfer to gentile authorities....

Hence, in response to the question, it is clear and simple that every Jew is forbidden to take part in any action which might facilitate the evacuation of a settlement, [military] camp or installation. As Maimonides ruled... even if the king gives an order to transgress the words of the *Torah*, we do not listen to him."

There exist two alternative prognoses of the practical effect which this rabbinical statement is likely to exert: one minimalist; the other maximalist. Cautiously optimistic, the minimalist position rests on assessments that the dimensions of religiously-inspired conscientious objection amongst IDF servicemen and women to a withdrawal from the territories will remain within easily manageable proportions. In the last resort, it argues, the vast majority of religious troops, including *besder* troops, are far more likely to obey the orders of their immediate military superiors than the instructions of their rabbinical mentors.

Prominent among those who tends towards a minimalist assessment, at least in public, are several senior officers in the IDF. [29] In part, their position is based on intimate familiarity with the psychology of conscripts, the vast majority of whom (in Israel as elsewhere) are conditioned to submit almost automatically to military discipline. This generic assertion is

---

[29] See, e.g., statements by Brig.-General Ilan Birn (CO Central Command), reported in *Davar* (Tel-Aviv, Hebrew daily), 11 August 1995 and by Brig.-General Yoram Yair, outgoing head of Manpower Branch, *Ha-Aretz*, 28 August 1995. Both officers warned that they would instigate severe measures against troops who refused orders, but doubted whether many instances would occur.

reinforced by the observation that the rabbinical statement was in any case signed by just a handful of *besder* principals — and immediately condemned by several others.[30] Moreover, the manifesto generated an extended and public intra-rabbinic debate conducted in the pages of *Ha-Tzofeh* (the national-religious daily) and *Nekudah* (the monthly journal of the Jewish settlers in Judea, Samaria and the Gaza Strip), silenced only by the trauma of Rabin's assassination. With positions at the apex of religious Zionist opinion so clearly divided, it has been suggested, the grass roots reaction is likely to be confused. Orders to dismantle military installations or even Jewish settlements, although undoubtedly liable to be distasteful to many troops, will probably be disobeyed on religious grounds by only a small minority. Fears of mass defections can therefore be dismissed. So too can apprehensions about a more violent form of national-religious military reaction.

The maximalist prognosis is considerably more alarmist. Basically, this is because it views the rabbinical call to military insubordination as a barometer of the temperature of the mainstream of contemporary national-religious thought, rather than an expression of a marginal current of opinion. From this perspective, then, the manifesto published in July 1995 in fact constitutes both a symptom and a warning. It is a symptom because it emerges from a societal background of growing disenchantment with the capacity of the IDF to embody values which the national religious community considers sublime. It is a warning because the manifesto concretizes a feeling that only measures of a drastic nature can defend interests presently under threat. If correct, this analysis carries ominous implications. A refusal to obey military orders to dismantle in-

---

[30] One of the most prominent rabbinical leaders to condemn the manifesto was Rabbi Yehudah Amital, the joint head of one of the largest of the *yeshivot besder*, head of the centrist religious party *Meimad* and — after Rabin's assassination — a cabinet minister without portfolio. Y. Amital, "A Political Opinion in Halakhic Camouflage", *Meimad* (Hebrew), 5 (September 1995), pp. 3–8.

stallations or settlements, it implies, might denote just the first steps on a road which could eventually lead to far more active forms of defiance, however unconcerted and disorganized the form which they might take.

Hesdernicks might not necessarily be the only troops inclined to follow that route. But they could spearhead more widespread activity. One reason (already noted) lies in the intensity of their exposure to extra-military rabbinic influences, even during their terms of conscript service. Another, possibly even more potent, results from the tentacular nature of their ties of association, which extend long into their careers as reservists. With the possible exception of former Air Force pilots, *hesder* graduates comprise the most close-knit of all the Israeli "old-boys' networks" created by common service in the IDF. Several marry sisters of their comrades in arms; many form and attend synagogues of their own; once they establish families, a high percentage move (or return) to national-religious communities, some of which are located in Judea and Samaria. Hence, even when no longer attached to homogenous military units, *hesder* reservists continue to constitute a possible focus of disaffection, well-placed to stimulate a process in which their own role might thereafter amount to more of a trigger than the actual weapon of insubordination.

For what it is worth, my own opinion (based, inter alia, on extensive interviews with a sample of *hesder* reservists and conscripts) is that such apprehensions are exaggerated. *Hesder* graduates do not figure in disproportionate numbers amongst the reservists who have already declared their readiness to disobey summonses to duty rather than implement the Oslo accords.[31] Neither is there any evidence to suggest that *hesder* conscripts on active duty might adopt that position. Altogether, the maximalist prognosis seems excessively alarmist. Quite apart from overlooking wide differences of outlook which exist between various

---

[31] Nadav Shragai, "Who Will Refuse Orders?", *Ha-Aretz*, 7 September 1995.

yeshivot hesder (and, for that matter, within individual academies[32]), it also ignores the more specific military organizational constraints under which *hesder* conscripts labour when in uniform. Cohesive though they are, *hesder* units do not possess their own autonomous structure of immediate military command. Seldom larger than companies in size, they are very rarely (and never deliberately) lead by corporals, sergeants and second lieutenants who themselves graduated from the *hesder* ranks. Consequently, even at a relatively junior and core level, they might be assumed to lack the ingredient of formal leadership upon which all concerted military operations ultimately depend. More extensive action would seem to be precluded by the integration of *hesder* companies (in their various corps) into the wider divisional and batallion formations which control the logistic and communications facilities so essential for unit survival.

V

That said, the course of recent events nevertheless cautions against too sanguine an attitude towards the maximalist prognosis and its fears. Possibly, the assassination of Prime Minister Rabin in November 1995 by a *hesder* graduate can be dismissed as an aberration. Even so, there remain three other phenomena which command attention as omens of crisis between the national-religious community and the IDF. In an ascending scale of severity they may be summarily categorized as: (i) circumvention; (ii) defamation; and (iii) confrontation.

Circumvention is limited entirely to the Jewish settler community and takes the form of the maintenance of a local security apparatus quite independent of the framework which the IDF itself supplies. Ever since 1979, settlers have operated

---

[32] On which see: Eliezer Don-Yehiya, "The Nationalist Yeshivot and Political Radicalism in Israel", in: M. E. Marty and R. Scott Appleby (eds.), *Accounting for Fundamentalism* (Chicago: Chicago University Press, 1994), pp. 264–302.

their own system of armed highway patrols, emergency res-
cue-services and perimeter guards.[33] Although originally set up
with the encouragement of the regional military authorities,
who issued the required licenses for citizens to bear arms, such
networks gained increasing autonomy during the *intifadah*,
when the protection provided by local IDF forces often seemed
inadequate to settler needs. The 1995 Tabah accords, which
mandate a contraction in the IDF's presence on the West Bank,
further stimulated that development. Settlers now look to
organizations bearing such resonant titles as *Ha-Shomer* ("The
Guardian") or *Shomer Yisrael* ("Israel's Guardian") to provide
them with the personal protection which, in palmier days, they
expected to receive from the Israeli military authorities. Whether
or not the self-defence networks thus created might comprise
the embryonic nucleus of a "Greater Israel" militia of vigilantes
must remain an open question.[34] At the very least, they give
practical expression to a lack of confidence in the IDF's ability
to guarantee the settlers' safety. In the words of one local rabbinic
directive:

"We do entrust the armed forces with general responsibility for our welfare. But anyone
face to face with an attack will have to mobilize his own initiative and training, since
we are commanded [by God] not to trust in miracles."[35]

While in many quarters of settler opinion discontent has bred
a sense of detachment from Israel's armed forces, in others it
has also facilitated their **defamation**. The most explicit evidence for this phenomenon comes from the periodical literature
published by Jewish settlers in Judea, Samaria and the Gaza
Strip, a survey of which reveals a steady intensification in both

---

[33] On the origins, see: Danny Rubinstein, *On the Lord's Side: Gush Emunim* (Tel-
Aviv: Ha-Kibbutz Ha-Meuchad, 1982), pp. 96–97. For later reports: *Yediot Aharonot*,
30 June 1995 and *Ha-Tzofeh* 11 July 1995.
[34] According to one report, the IDF Education Corps commissioned a study of the
subject immediately after the first Oslo accords (*Ha-Aretz*, 19 November 1993).
[35] Rabbi Daniel Shiloh of the Kedumim settlement, in *Bulletin of West Bank Rabbis*,
(Hebrew), 30 (winter 1995–6), p. 3.

the derogatory tone and critical content of opinion on IDF conduct.[36] During the early stages of the *intifadah*, most expressions of settler dissatisfaction had been directed against the government, which was broadly accused of keeping local IDF commanders on a political leash. The IDF's apparent inability to put an end to Palestinian assaults on settler persons and property, however, soon generated a shift in target. By the end of 1991, the settlers were openly calling for the replacement of the Chief of Staff, claiming that no other measure would restore the IDF's self-assurance.[37] News that the entire General Staff had helped to negotiate both the Cairo accords of 1994 and the Tabah agreement of 1995, precipitated a broadening of the objects of settler disdain. The staff of Central Command (within whose domain of jurisdiction most setters lie) were lampooned with especial regularity; at the same time, the IDF as a whole was accused of being pusillanimous. Another symbolic threshold was reached — and crossed — some time before the rabbinic manifesto of July 1995. Ever since 1994, the most strident of settler spokesmen had begun to deny the right of the military to be regarded as the incarnation of the true "national spirit". Instead, they portrayed the Israel Defense Force (in Hebrew: *Tzevah Haganah le-Yisrael*) as the "Israel Defeatist Army" (*Tzevah Tevusah le-Yisrael*), and denigrated its senior officers as local versions of Marshal Petain.[38]

In their most extreme version, such accusations remain the views of a minority. An opinion survey which I conducted in the winter of 1995 revealed that almost 75% of Jewish settlers still express deep respect for the IDF and pride in its

---

[36] These sources are reviewed in Ze'ev Schiff, "The IDF has been Removed from the National Consensus", *Ha-Aretz*, 2 June 1995.

[37] E.g., Eliezer Melamed, "The End of the Period of Restraint", *Nekudah*, 82. (December 1991), pp. 22–3.

[38] For a sample of the most strident examples see: Elyakim Ha-Etzni, "From a Defence Force to a Force of Abandonment", *Nekudah*, 175 (Feb. 1994), pp. 22–24; and interview with Zvi Katzover, the head of Kiryat Arba local council, in *Ma'ariv*, 24 March 1995.

achievements.[39] On a day-to-day basis, individual IDF troops who come into contact with the settlers similarly experience overwhelming support (usually, and most materially, expressed by the regular provision of gifts of home-made cookies to locally stationed servicemen). Nevertheless, changes in the undercurrent of mood cannot be ignored. In more diluted renditions, expressions of settler disdain have already begun to filter into wider segments of national-religious opinion. They are regularly reprinted in *Ha-Tzofeh* (the daily newspaper funded by the National-Religious Party — *Mafdal*) and echoed in the *kneset* by spokesmen for national-religious opinion. More significantly still, they have also permeated B'nei Akiva (the most popular of the national-religious youth movements; above p. 82), which at its 1995 annual conference adopted a resolution which implicitly supported the right to conscientious objection on the grounds that withdrawal from the Land of Israel contravened Divine law.[40] Together, these tendencies portend substantive shifts in the overwhelmingly affirmative attitude towards military service which, as we have seen, used to be one of the national-religious community's most distinctive characteristics. Indeed, they suggest that a process of de-legitimization might be steadily undermining the almost mythological reverence which the IDF once enjoyed, especially amongst this sector.

That impression is confirmed when attention is turned, finally, to the still more drastic phenomenon of **confrontation**. For many years, scenarios of possible Jewish settler violence (influenced by the discovery of a militant Jewish "underground" in 1985) portrayed the local Arab population as the most likely victims of potential attack.[41] A shift of focus might now be

---

[39] Contrast, however, the findings of an earlier survey conducted by the settlers themselves, who claim that less than 60% of their community objected in principle to violent opposition to their withdrawal. *Nekudah*, 180 (September 1994), p. 48.

[40] *Zeraim* (B'nei Akiva journal; Hebrew), 8 (August 1995), p. 6.

[41] The literature is summarized in: Ian S. Lustick, *For the Land and the Lord* (New

required. Even before the first Oslo agreement of September 1993, the frequency with which IDF troops were being despatched to disperse settler demonstrations gave rise to predictions that the two sides were set on "a collision course".[42] Since that watershed, potential areas of friction have steadily widened. In 1994 and 1995, settler leaders — many of whom early in 1994 formed an "Actions Committee for the Annulment of the Autonomy Plan"[43] — evinced a growing readiness to initiate such acts of civil disobedience as sit-ins and road closures. For their part, the police and IDF authorities displayed equal determination to deploy large numbers of personnel in order to maintain law and order. It is a tribute to the mutual restraint exercised by both sides that the consequent clashes did not lead to casualties. They were, however, marked by a process of escalation, and moved along a trajectory which began with heated verbal exchanges, proceeded to physical (albeit non-violent) tussles and culminated in large-scale arrests.[44]

There exists no authoritative index of the influence which the developments outlined above might be exerting on national religious troops in general, and on *hesder* units in particular. Taken together, however, individual items of information give pause for sober thought. One disturbing sign, for instance, is the prominent role played in settler confrontations with IDF troops by pre-conscript youngsters, many of whom are members of B'nei Akiva, from whose ranks most *hesder* pupils are drawn. This circumstance gives rise to conjecture that many *hesder* troops might enter military service with a personal record of an adversarial relationship with the force into which they

---

York: Council on Foreign Relations, 1988) and David Weisburd, *Jewish Settler Violence: Deviance as Social Reaction* (Pennsylvania: Pennsylvania State University Press, 1989).

[42] Ze'ev Schiff, "Settlers against the IDF", *Ha-Aretz*, 17 June 1992.

[43] Report on IDF radio, 10 March 1994. Transcript in *Foreign Broadcasting Information Service* NES–94–048, p. 21.

[44] The Israeli press carried lengthy reports of such incidents. See: e.g., *Ha-Aretz*, 14 July 1995.

are being drafted. It also places clearly defined limits on the operational uses to which such troops might be put. As early as December 1993, several members of a *hesder* unit were tried — and sentenced — by a military court for not displaying the required degree of animation when dispersing settler demonstrations.[45] In what can only be interpreted as a determination to avoid similar incidents, the IDF thereafter noticeably refrained from employing *hesder* troops on such operations. Instead, such tasks are now assigned to "special units", composed (according to some reports) of military and police personnel whose religious and political affiliations have presumably been carefully vetted.[46]

Should it be extended, that particular "arrangement" threatens to undermine the basis upon which the *hesder* was originally founded. More seriously still, it will impinge upon the integrative ethos which has traditionally been a source of IDF pride. Therein, it is here suggested, lies the ultimate (and most ironic) feature of the situation which the *hesder* programme presently confronts. In themselves, the *hesder* units can hardly be portrayed as a military threat to Israeli democracy or to the liberal principle of governmental control over the armed forces. Their importance lies elsewhere. By their existence, they bring to the fore tensions between military service and religious obligations in a particularly acute form. Hence, they generate reactions (and fears) which in turn exacerbate the divisions to which Israeli society is in any case prone.

---

[45] *Ha-Tzofeh*, 21 December 1993.
[46] *Ha-Aretz*, 7 October 1994 and *Yediot Aharonot* 25 Nov. 1994 and 6 August 1995.

Afterword

Cynics sometimes remark that if all the words written about the religious-secular divide in Israel were laid out end to end, they still would not bridge the communal chasm. This book cannot claim to refute that observation. Its aim has been to call attention to a dimension of social strife which, although often overlooked in the academic literature, nevertheless clamours for attention. Dilemmas between religious beliefs and military service, it has sought to show, now constitute a major item on the Israeli national agenda, intruding upon both the personal allegiances of individual troops and the institutional perceptions of military and political planners. Instead of being a "nation builder", military service in the IDF now threatens to become a great "nation divider", separating those who view the country's armed forces as the embodiment of the Zionist ethos from others who recognize alternative sources of authority and esteem.

Understandably sensitive to the paramount strategic importance of preserving cohesion within the ranks, IDF force planners seek to moderate the potentially corrosive effects of religious-secular discord — as of any other. One, traditional, way of doing so is by steadfastly projecting an image of institutional impartiality, which in practical terms translates into a disinclination to express corporate opinions on sensitive subjects of public debate, especially when coloured by an emotive admixture of religion and politics. More innovative has been the formulation of what is colloquially termed an IDF "code of ethics". After protracted consultations with both the academic community and senior military staff, the Education Corps in June 1995 unveiled *The Spirit of the IDF: Values and Basic Rules*. Comprising 177 pages of original text, and a supplementary volume of eight suggested "readings", the document itemizes eleven basic IDF values and thirty-four additional norms. It also contains an educational "kit", intended to provide commanders with guidelines and to serve as a work of reference for specific lectures on individual themes.

The very fact that a "code" of military ethics had to be formulated, and published, itself bears testimony to the severity of the problems which *The Spirit of the IDF* seeks to alleviate. After all, and as the authors explicitly state in their own introduction, the document makes no claim to originality. It merely summarizes the principles of conduct to which the Force has supposedly always adhered (e.g. "responsibility", "the purity of arms", "collegiality", "professionalism", etc.). What has changed, rather, is the general societal ambience which once made such norms self-evident. Some aspects of IDF behaviour during the *intifadah*, especially, emphasized the need to codify core values and make them more explicit. The trauma which the peace process might engender, likewise, heightens the urgency of specifying a common denominator of comportment. Finally, and of most immediate relevance to the subject of the present book, so too does the perceptibly widening gap between the perceptions and attitudes of many religious and secular troops.

In conformity with a long-standing IDF tradition (above, chapter 2), *The Spirit of the IDF* attempts to address the religious-secular divide by invoking the homogenizing referents of a common past. Hence, it specifies the "traditions of the Jewish people throughout the ages" as the very first of the "roots" of the principles subsequently elaborated. That mode of expression might have been appropriate in an earlier age, when relations between religious and secular troops were still usually cordial and when attitudes towards security policies were still overwhelmingly consensual. But in the social and political circumstances now prevailing, it is doubtful whether so amorphous a nod in the direction of "tradition" can effectively appeal to either camp.[1]

---

[1] For national religious disdain of both the text and its principal author, see: e.g., Meirah Dolev, "Asa Kasher's Impure Document" *Nekudah*, 184 (Feb. 1995), pp. 28–31.

Not even all national-religious Jews in Israel now sense an automatic and universal affinity with their non-religious fellow-citizens.[2] Neither, on the other hand, do all secular Israelis regard the religious community — including the Zionist religious community — as common partners in the opportunity for national reconstruction which they believe the peace process to have made possible.

Furthermore, the need to publish *The Spirit of the IDF* also appears to underscore a vulnerability that is institutional as well as ideological. In many basic essentials, of which the most salient is its increasing drive towards "professionalization", the present IDF is almost the converse of the Force which Israelis once knew. As such, it is less well-equipped (and certainly less eager) to play the role of the melting pot in which it was cast by Ben-Gurion. In such spheres as education, land settlement, immigrant absorption — all critical components of traditional Zionist values — the military contribution to societal causes has shrivelled almost to obscurity. At the same time, the IDF has been deprived of some of its mythological social status. The implications of that background for relations between religious and secular troops are particularly severe. Within each community, and often for different reasons, criticism of the IDF has assumed a life of its own, cumulative and self-re-enforcing. In national-religious society, the trend has taken a particularly ominous form.

How the compound cluster of circumstances outlined in this book might affect the attitude of the military authorities in Israel towards religious troops under their command remains to be seen. Already apparent, however, are the effects on religious personnel themselves. Confronted with the reality of conflict between their theological beliefs and their patriotic duty, the

---

[2] Thus, in the survey of high school students noted above (p. 59; table YG 27), some 45% of the religious respondents said they felt themselves more "Jewish" than "Israeli" (almost double the figure in the secular segment).

accommodations once worked out in order to harmonize the scroll and the sword now seem inadequate. Instead of being compatible entities, they now — as taught so long ago by Rabbi Eleazar of Modi'in — increasingly appear to be antagonistic alternatives.

Index

Abrabanel, Don Isaac 19
Amalek 13–14, 91
Amital, Yehudah 81 fn 20, 132 fn 30

Babylonian Talmud
cited: x, 7 fn 10, 12 fn 19, 13 fn 20, 32 fn 47, 92, 97, 99, fn 41, 42, 100, 101 fn 47
Bar Kokhba 2, 5–6
Barkai 24
Be'er, Haim 62
Begin, Menachem 27, 65
Ben-Gurion, David
grant of deferments to service 86; opposition to separate religious units 43–45, 105; vision of IDF 41, 123
B'TSELEM 127
Bible
cited: x, xii, 2, 9, 13, 19, 32, 47, 85, 89, 91, 93, 98 fn 41, 99; exegesis on 4, 91; presented to new recruits 54, 56–57; warfare in 1
B'nei Akiva 60, 82–83, 129, 137–138
"Buddy syndrome" 71, 119

Civic service programmes 66–67, 93
Civil-military relations 124–126
Conscientious objection 126–128
"Court of 71" 18–20, 26, 35

Dayan, Mosheh 108
Drori, Ya'akov 107
Druze troops in IDF 45, 110

Enlistment
national status of 74–77; national-religious attitudes towards 78–85; ultra-orthodox attitudes towards 94–101; *see also:* Non-enlistment

Federation of *Yeshivot Hesder* 109, 114
Female military service
legislation 40, 66–67, 112 fn 6; national-religious attitudes towards 93; ultra-orthodox attitudes towards 87, 92–93
Friedman, Menachem 90

Goldwicht, Hayyim 106–108, 123
Goren, Shlomo 56, 65–66, 129; cited: 13 fn 21, 24, 26 fn 38
Gush Emunim 82

Ha-Levi, Judah 5
Ha-Torah ve-Ha-Medinah 24
Ha-Rabbanut Ha-Tzeva'it
decline in status of 61–62; duties 47–48; education programmes 51–52; establishment of 45–46; prerogatives 49–50; structure and status 46–47
Ha-Tzofeh 132, 137

Haganah 43
Haredim, see: Ultra-orthodox
community.
Harkabi, Yehoshafat 5
Hazon Ish 23, 89
Herzl, Theodore 7
Herzog, Isaac 22–23, 25; cited
5 fn 24
Hesder units in IDF 63
as military organizations 134; as
"old boys' network" 133; as
threat to civilian
government 131–134; conditions
of service in 111–114;
establishment of 105–109;
military opinions of 118–122;
national-religious community
and 115–118; officer recruitment
in 121–122; public standing
of 122–124.
·Horowitz, Dan 58

Intifadah (1987–1993) xv, 16, 27,
127, 136, 142
Israel Defense Forces (IDF)
battle motivation in 72; Ben-
Gurion's view of 41–42; "code
of ethics" 141–142; composition
and structure of 40–41, 75–6;
condition of service in 112–114;
conscientious objection in
126–128; domestic status of
xiv–vi, 76–77; *mador
beinish* 110; oath of
allegiance 64; "professionalism"
in 57–58,
74–75; rabbinate, see: *ha-
rabbanut ha-tzeva'it;* religious
observance in 48–50; religious

troops in 84–85; "role
expansion" of 38–39; settler
community and 134–138; use of
religious symbols 52–54

Joshua 13
"Just wars" 10; See also: *Milkhemet
mitzvah*

Karelitz, Abraham Yeshayahu *see:*
"Hazon Ish"
Kerem be-Yavneh academy 107
Kook, Abraham Isaac 25, 79–80,
89
Kook academy (Jerusalem) 81 fn
19, 102, 129
Kook, Zvi Yehudah 80, 93, 117

Land of Israel
conquest of by Joshua 13;
religious duty to defend 32;
religious opposition to
withdrawal from 31, 65,
128–131, 137; ultra-orthodox
attitude towards 94–95
Lebanon War (1982–1985) xv, 119,
126
Liechtenstein, Aaron 116 fn 9
Lipkin-Shahak, Amnon 77

Maccabees 2 fn 3
Mador Beinish 110
MAFDAL *see:* National-Religious
Party.
Maimonides 8–15, 18–21, 29–30,
32–33, 98, 100–101, 130, 131
Marks, Richard 6
Mekhinot Kedam Tzevai'ot 63, 83,
84, 116 fn 10

Merkaz Harav Kook
  see: Kook academy (Jerusalem)
Military service
  status of in Israel xiv–vi, 76–7,
  141
Milkhemet mitzvah ("obligatory
  war") and *milkhemet reshut*
  ("discretionary war")
  definitions 15; distinctions
  between 11–24; examples of 13,
  16, 33; precedence in strategic
  planning 12–17; process of
  decision-making 21; service
  in 91–92

Nachmanides 31
NAHAL (Youth Pioneer
  Fighting) Corps
  form of enlistment in 45, 107,
  110; purposes 39
National-Religious Party 27, 122,
  137; attitude towards separate
  enlistment (1948–9) 43; *See also:*
  religious Zionists
Navon, Gad 56, 62
Nekudah 132
Non-enlistment
  by religious females 66–67; by
  religious males 67–68, 87

Operation Litani (1978) 17
Orr, Orri 123–124
Ostfeld, Zahavah 43

Palmach 44, 123
Peace Process xvi–xvii, 128, 142;
  impact on religious discourse
  concerning warfare 26–27,
  30–36, 65–66

Peron, Mordechai 56
Pikuah Nefesh ("saving of life");
  preferable to ceding
  territory 32–35

Rabin Yitzchak
  assassination of 57, 124, 134;
  government of 29, 128
Ravitzky, Aviezer 81
Religious observance in the
  IDF 48–50
Religious-secular divide amongst
  Israeli youth 59–61, 143
Religious troops in IDF
  attitude towards service 61–68,
  84–85
Religious units in IDF, see: *Hesder*
Religious Zionism
  foundation xi; pre-State attitudes
  towards uses of force 28;
  principles of 78–79
Religious Zionists
  "affirmative" attitudes towards
  enlistment 78–85; evidence of
  "resistant" attitude 102–104,
  117–118
Responsa literature 3 fn 5, 21–22,
  130
Rolbant, Samuel 55, 71

Sabbath Observance 32–33; in
  IDF 49–50
Saving of Life
  see: *pikuah nefesh*
Self-defence
  Zionist attitude towards 7–8
Settlements and settler community
  attitudes toward IDF 134–139
Shach, Eliezer 90, 93, 96

Shapira, Anita 8
Shiluv 116 fn 10
Sinai Campaign (1956) 17, 106
Six Days' War (1967) xv, 17, 26,
  54, 106; impact on religious
  Zionist thought 80–81

Tehumin 24
Torah-study, as supreme
  virtue 96–103, 116

Ultra-orthodox (*haredi*) Jewry
  growth and organization of
  86–87; emphasis on *Torah*-
  scholarship 96–103; "resistant"
  attitude towards enlistment
  85–101

"Union of Rabbis on Behalf of the
  People of Israel and the Land of
  Israel" 129–131

War of Independence (1948–9) 16
Warfare, traditional Jewish
  attitude towards 4–5; in
  Maimonidean code 9–21;
  modern Jewish teachings
  on 21–26; See also:
  milkhemet mitzvah

Yamit 27
Yesh Gevul 127
Yom Kippur War; (October
  1973) xv, 16, 53, 68, 81
Yosef, Ovadiah 34–35

For Product Safety Concerns and Information please contact our EU
representative GPSR@taylorandfrancis.com Taylor & Francis Verlag GmbH,
Kaufingerstraße 24, 80331 München, Germany

Batch number: 08153776

Printed by Printforce, the Netherlands